The Trial of
Slobodan Milosevic

Michael Barratt Brown
Edward S. Herman & David Peterson

SPOKESMAN
For
SOCIALIST RENEWAL

First published in 2004 by
Spokesman
Russell House, Bulwell Lane
Nottingham
NG6 0BT
Phone 0115 970 8318   Fax 0115 942 0433.
e-mail elfeuro@compuserve.com
www.spokesmanbooks.com
©Michael Barratt Brown
©Edward S. Herman and David Peterson

All rights reserved. No part of this publicaton may be reproduced, stored in a retrieval system or tansmitted in any form or by means, electronic, mechanical, photocopying, recording or otherwise, without the prior permission of the publishers.

ISBN 0 85124 693 1

A CIP catalogue is available from the British Library.

Printed by the Russell Press Ltd (phone 0115 978 4505)

Contents

I The Trial of Slobodan Milosevic
   by Michael Barratt Brown   5

II A Study in Propaganda
   by Edward S. Herman & David Peterson   31

The Trial of Slobodan Milosevic

Michael Barratt Brown

This essay is based on a careful reading of all 30,000 pages of the official transcripts up to the end of Febraury 2004 of the proceedings of the International Criminal Tribunal for Former Yugoslavia (ICTY) in the case of Slobodan Milosevic. Page numbers in brackets refer to these transcripts.

On most working days between September 2002 and February 2004, a visitor could enter a court-house in The Hague and observe the trial of the former elected President of Yugoslavia, the Serb leader Slobodan Milosevic. The visitor would see on the bench an English presiding judge, Judge Richard May, flanked by judges respectively from Jamaica and Sri Lanka. On the left, the prosecution is led by a gentleman enjoying the name of Mr. Nice. In the centre stand the witnesses brought by the prosecution. On the right, Milosevic is accompanied by a guard, but without defence lawyers, only two so-called *amici*, appointed by the court as 'friends' of the defendant without his consent. At the back of the court in boxes sit the stenographers and the translators – official translators of English, French and Serbo-Croatian and others from other countries. Above them a large screen is used for projecting images of photographs and documents presented as evidence of the criminal activities for which Milosevic has been indicted. For this is the main court-room of the UN International Criminal Tribunal for Former Yugoslavia (ICTY).

By March 2004, there had been nearly 300 court days and over 300 witnesses to testify at this trial and to be cross-questioned by Milosevic. And the trial of Milosevic is not the only one with which the International Criminal Court for Former Yugoslavia is concerned. In other rooms in the court-house other Serbs would be facing trial for crimes for which they have been indicted in connection with the civil wars in Croatia and Bosnia between 1991 and 1995 and in Kosovo in 1998-9. Occasionally, the indicted Serbs will be joined by an indicted Croat or a Muslim.

Most visitors entering the court will have pre-conceived ideas of what to expect. Milosevic, they will perhaps see as he is often depicted, a second Hitler who seized power in Yugoslavia as a Serb with the aim of creating a Greater Serbia and carrying out the 'ethnic cleansing' of Bosnia-Hercegovina, Kosovo and parts of Croatia. To this end his Serb army is said to have driven out of their homes hundreds of thousands who were not Serbs, but were Croats, Muslims and Albanians and to have murdered many thousands who had resisted. This was supposedly but the last stage of a barbaric history in which the different ethnic groups in the country had fought each other over the ages, only restrained by outside imperial powers – Turks, Italians, Hungarians, Austrians, Germans – and most recently by the iron hand of Marshal Tito. After much hesitation, so the story ends, the international community had at length sent NATO forces into the country to stop the fighting, ensure the independence of the Slovenes, the Croats, the Bosnians and the protection of the Kosovars and to bring Milosevic to trial. It makes a good story, but is it true?

The documents circulated at the court state the terms of the indictment:

> 'Slobodan Milosevic is individually criminally responsible for the crimes referred to in Articles 2,3,4 and 5 of the Statute of this Tribunal as described in this indictment, which he planned, instigated, ordered, committed, or in whose planning, preparation, or execution he otherwise aided and abetted. By using the word 'committed' in this indictment, the Prosecutor does not intend to suggest that the accused physically committed any of the crimes charged personally. 'Committed' in this indictment refers to participation in a joint criminal enterprise as a co-perpetrator.'

The 'joint criminal enterprise' included charges of 'genocide or complicity in genocide' – 'the destruction in whole or in part, of the Bosnian Muslim and Bosnian Croat national, ethnical, racial or religious groups as such, in territories within Bosnia and Hercegovina', as well as 'crimes against humanity, grave breaches of the Geneva Conventions and violations of the laws and customs of war in Bosnia Hercegovina, Croatia and Kosovo.'

A visitor who wishes to remain impartial and listen closely to the proceedings to reach his or her own judgement would have to bear in mind that there is another view that is not so widely held, but has much evidence to support it. On this view, the several, mainly Slav, peoples of Yugoslavia had lived together in peace for hundreds of years, except when they were invaded by Turks, Hungarians, Austrians, Italians, Germans and now Americans; that Tito's Partisans, drawn from all the several Yugoslav communities, had held down more German and Axis divisions in Yugoslavia in World War Two than the British and American forces had done at the same time in North Africa or in Italy; that Tito's rule in peacetime was not a military dictatorship but a federation of peoples with large elements of political and economic democracy; that the country began to fall apart even before Tito's death because of demands made on it, as on many other developing countries, by the institutions of international capital, the International Monetary Fund and American Banks; that the first acts of civil war came from Slovenia and Croatia, not from Serbia; that Milosevic was an elected President, whom the Americans called on to underwrite the peace in Bosnia Hercegovina; that the numbers killed in the civil war have been greatly exaggerated; that it was mainly Serbs who were driven out of their homes in Bosnia and Croatia and that the 'protection' of Kosovo has driven most Serbs out of their homes there; but it has left the Americans with a massive military base in Kosovo, 'Camp Bondsteel'.

On this view, the main responsibility for the break-up of Yugoslavia and the subsequent civil wars lies with outside forces, primarily German and American, who fought out their own rivalry on the bodies of the Yugoslav peoples. This is the view which this author believes to be true on the basis of many years' experience in Former Yugoslavia. It is a view shared by many who have wide experience in Former Yugoslavia, including most particularly two authors: Susan Woodward, who worked in Zagreb in 1987-90, from which her book *The Political Economy of Yugoslavia, 1945-90* (Princeton 1995) derived, and was the special assistant to the chief UN representative in Bosnia in 1994, from which experience came her *Balkan Tragedy* (Brookings 1995); and Diana Johnstone, whose book *Fools' Crusade* (Pluto Press 2002) is based on the most careful study of the evidence in the Milosevic trial..

But we must return to our imaginary visitor at the Milosevic trial before the International Criminal Court for Former Yugoslavia, to help him or her to understand what is going on. The visitor will indeed be observing an historic event. This is a new form of trial. It is the first international trial of an elected head of state and of his accomplices since the Nuremberg trials of Hitler's associates. The trial before an international court of a UN indicted war criminal has created an important precedent, which might be followed in the cases of others. Although the Yugoslav government at the time had expressed the wish to try Milosevic themselves, after his defeat in the elections of 2000, he was 'lifted' out of Belgrade to The Hague by NATO armed personnel. To be named an 'indicted war criminal' already carried an assumption of guilt.

Under an agreement of May 9th 1996, NATO had been made the official gendarme for the Tribunal. The methods employed in bringing prisoners to The Hague for trial has raised some questions about human rights. Special US armed units and others attracted by the very large rewards offered for a capture were employed to kidnap indicted Serbs, with instructions to shoot them if they resisted. Several examples were given by Diana Johnstone in her book *Fool's Crusade*, taken from newspaper reports of indicted Serbs being shot when they tried to escape arrest and of others dying in their cells in The Hague. Slavko Dokmanovic, one time mayor of Vukovar, was indicted and seized in 1997 for trial for executing 250 Croat soldiers from a hospital in Vukovar in November of 1991. He was able to prove that he had been elsewhere at the time, and should have been acquitted, but was found dead in his cell in June 1998. Milosevic made much of such cases in his opening address at the second part of the trial, concerned with Croatia and Bosnia (pages 11027 ff.). Jilan Milutinovic, President of Serbia under Milosevic, gave himself up for reasons that are not clear, when his term of office came to an end and was taken to The Hague to face the Tribunal by which he had been indicted.

What may have happened to Milutinovic is suggested by the story of what happened to Radovan (Ratko) Markovic, Milosevic's chief of state security. He was taken out of Belgrade where he was in jail and brought to The Hague. It had been expected that his evidence would finally pin the blame on Milosevic for 'ethnic cleansing' in Kosovo. A

The Trial of Slobodan Milosevic

special Jeremy Paxman programme had been organised on BBC TV for July 26th 2002 to publicise this, but things did not turn out as expected. Markovic told the Tribunal that he had been tortured and offered asylum if he witnessed that he had committed criminal acts on the orders of Milosevic. In the event, in answer to examination he refused to do so, and said that the instructions fell entirely within the laws of war (page 8765). It is a surprising aspect of the Tribunal's methods of work that the judge did not stop the proceedings and call for an inquiry into the truth of this allegation of torture. Markovic was returned to jail in Belgrade. In February 24th. 2004 he retracted in a Belgrade court the further confession he had made earlier under promises of protection for himself and his family, of involvement in the death of Ivan Stambolic. Stambolic was a much loved one time Serb President and protector of Milosevic, whom Milosevic had turned against to further his own ambitions.

The status of this court has at all appropriate times, and some inappropriate times, been challenged by Milosevic. The comparison is often made in the world media, comparing Milosevic and the Serb armies with Hitler and the Nazis and of the Hague trials with the Nuremberg trials. Milosevic ridicules this. In a civil war his forces never left Yugoslavia. It was NATO forces from outside that attacked a sovereign state. He denies that he gave orders for illegal actions or knowingly failed to prevent them. He insists that in both Nuremberg and The Hague, it is victors' justice that rules. Indeed, he frequently complains that judge and prosecution (there is no jury) all come from NATO countries which invaded his country without UN sanction. He points to evidence that most of the pressure for the trials comes from outside the country. There is much support for his view.

The first chief prosecutor at the Tribunal (ICTY) was Richard Goldstone, a South African whose reputation came from his experience in the post-apartheid Truth and Reconciliation Commission. He did not reappear when the trial of Milosevic began, but before he left, he compared what he called 'the Bosnian victims' desire for revenge' with the South African blacks' satisfaction with the Truth Commission, suggesting that this was because of the greater degree of crime in Bosnian genocide. By contrast, David Chandler in his book *Bosnia: Faking Democracy after Dayton* (Pluto Press 2000), based on a long period of study in Bosnia, concluded that 'The ICTY has little support within Bosnia... Poll findings show that for Bosnian people of all three groups the question of war crimes is of little importance. Accusations of war crimes, so far, seem to have done little to develop community reconciliation.' And there was no sign of that happening in the following years

A New International Court

The history of the establishment of the International Criminal Tribunal for Former Yugoslavia is interesting. It was the particular child of both German and American foreign policy. Klaus Kinkel, the German Foreign Minister in August 1992, called for a tribunal to prosecute the Serbs for genocide. This was following the outbreak of fighting in Slavonia (a largely Serb populated part of Croatia) between Croat forces and the Yugoslav Peoples' Army (JNA), which was even at that time predominantly Serb officered. When the Tribunal's first president, Antonio Casese, was nominated, he referred to Kinkel as 'the father of the Tribunal'. The idea of a Yugoslav tribunal had received essential support, in 1993, after the United States government first became involved in the Yugoslav civil war. Casese's successor, Gabrielle Kirk Mc Donald, described Madeline Albright, President Clinton's Secretary of State, as the 'mother of the Tribunal', commenting that 'she had worked with unceasing resolve to establish the Tribunal' with the Serbs as its main quarry. Mrs Albright had instructed Michael Scharf to draft the Tribunal's statute. At the time it was given a low profile. In commenting on it later, Scharf wrote (*Washington Post*, October 3, 1999), that the Tribunal was 'widely perceived within government as little more than a public relations device ... and useful policy tool... Indictments would serve to isolate offending leaders diplomatically and fortify the international political will to employ sanctions or use force.'

The Tribunal has no connection with the International Court of Justice, set up by the United Nations, or with the International Criminal Court, which is not recognised by the United States, at least for its citizens. Milosevic again and again in his trial insists on the fact that the Tribunal has no legal basis under the UN Charter. He has some justification. The UN Security Council did set up the Tribunal, but under Chapter Seven of the Charter, which grants the Council power to 'take measures' and 'establish subsidiary bodies' in the interest of maintaining 'peace and security' (some would question that!). Under its statute, the Tribunal's expenses were supposed to come out of the UN budget, but in fact it has depended on US and other governments' funding, on donations from George Soros and other private donors, with equipment and staff seconded by NATO members. Some $3 million came from the United States in 1994-5, when the US was failing to meet its financial obligations to the United Nations. Gilbert Guillaume, President of the International Court of Justice, complained to the UN General Assembly in October 2000 that the Tribunal got ten times more money than his court and suggested that this was because 'various parties create new forums that will be more amenable to their arguments.' 'Kangaroo courts' he might have called them.

In the court Milosevic stands alone with his guard behind him. He has no counsel, just his two *amici*, who ask questions to clarify points in the prosecution's case. One at least does not seem to be such a good friend. Milosevic had to complain (page 10317) that the *amicus* Mr Wladimiroff had written an article in a Bulgarian journal, *Kultura*, that if Milosevic was not caught on one count he would be convicted on others 'like any animal pursued in a hunt for game', as he rather crudely put it. Milosevic has insisted on defending himself. At one stage he was pressed to accept as his defence counsel Ramsay Clark, an ex-US Attorney General, who had been an outspoken critic of US actions in Yugoslavia. Milosevic would not have him, perhaps wisely. For Clark, while calling Milosevic a 'war criminal', has stated that he was acting for him, which appears not to be the case.

Milosevic has rather limited resources. He has a lawyer at The Hague to discuss each day's business with. He has the not always reliable use of a telephone in his prison to communicate with a back-up team – some of the team in Canada, most in Yugoslavia – who inform him and his lawyer of the background of each of the prosecution witnesses, whose written statements have been made available to him in advance of their hearing. He has often had to complain that witnesses appeared in the wrong order, that there were too many 'protected' (i.e. incognito) witnesses, and that the judge does not give him as long for cross-examination as the prosecutor had been allowed for examination. Evidence from General Wesley Clark was received in closed session at the insistence of the US Government, and the General was allowed to phone Bill Clinton in the middle of his statement to obtain confirmation of a point at issue.

Milosevic was not, in fact, indicted until 1999, just at the moment when NATO moved to an all out bombardment of Serbia proper from its more limited attacks on Yugoslav forces in Kosovo. This delay was not surprising because Milosevic had been called upon, in 1995, by the United States negotiators to underwrite the Dayton Accords, which ended the fighting in Bosnia. At first the Milosevic indictment was concerned only with crimes against humanity and violations of the laws or customs of war in Kosovo. But when it became clear, after 2001, that not half a million but 3,000 had been killed on both sides in Kosovo, and that Al Qaeda had close links with the Kosova Liberation Army, Carla del Ponte, the Prosecutor, decided to add to the indictment similar charges in Croatia and the more serious charge of genocide in Bosnia. She was the third prosecutor to be appointed and was said to show an almost embarrassing enthusiasm for what she called 'hunting down criminals' of the Bosnian war. It turned out that most of these were Serbs. Ms. Del Ponte's view was that Croats could be excused indictment because 'their own courts could deal with such matters'.

One indictment has not been considered, although a lengthy and carefully argued case was presented to the Tribunal by Canadian law professor Michael Mandel and a group of American lawyers, and that is an indictment of NATO for the bombing of Serbia in 1999 without UN authorisation. Ms del Ponte, in 2000 in a report reviewing the NATO bombing campaign (UN doc. PR/P.I.S./510 E), concluded that 'NATO and NATO countries' press statements are generally reliable and that explanations have been honestly given'. That egregious spin doctor Jamie Shea at a NATO press conference on May 17, 1999 said that he had no worries about prosecution. The prosecutor will start her investigation, 'because we will allow her to' and 'when she looks at the facts, she will be indicting people of Yugoslav nationality, and I don't anticipate any others at this stage.' Charles Trueheart in the *Washington Post* (20.01.2000) quoted NATO officials saying that 'they had been assured by Ms. Del Ponte that she would not carry that exercise far'. And she didn't.

Only One Side Charged – Why mainly Serbs, not Croats or Muslims?

A few leading Croats and Muslims as well as the many Serbs have been indicted for war crimes and brought for trial to The Hague – a small number of Croats and Muslims taking into account that there were many examples of actions by Croat forces in Gospic, in Eastern Slavonia, and in the Krajina, and by Muslim forces around Srebrenica, which would seem to be just as indictable as anything the Serbs were accountable for – in terms of sheer numbers being made to suffer, perhaps more indictable. A visitor to the Tribunal, or anyone reading the transcripts of the trials, is bound to ask why the difference. Fortunately for the Croats their leader Franjo Tudjman died before he could be arraigned as Milosevic's opposite number; and now the Muslim leader Alija Izetbegovic is dead. Milosevic is the great survivor, but for how long? He is an ill man and his trial seems likely to go on for many more months. Perhaps the hope of his prosecutors is that he will die before the Tribunal comes to make its judgment. In the event, despite Milosevic's continued illnesses, it is Judge May who has said that, because of ill health, he will have to retire in May of 2004, before Milosevic makes his final case for the defence.

Where leading Croats have been indicted there has been great difficulty in getting the Croatian government to hand over the indicted criminals. Even risking sanctions, the government refused to hand over General Janko Bobetko, but the general died before sanctions had to be imposed. The most senior Croat still wanted in 2003 for war crimes in Yugoslavia, General Ante Gotovina, appeared at that time to be the subject of complex negotiations between Carla del Ponte for the Tribunal, the Croatian government, the European Union and the British government. At issue was Croatia's application for membership of the European Union, which was being blocked by a British ultimatum that Gotovina be handed over to the Tribunal. The Croatian Prime Minister, Ivica Tucan, a Social Democrat and former Communist, was lobbying Tony Blair at the end of September

2003 to take a softer line. Gotovina had been on the run since 2001,when he was tipped off that he would be indicted. The Croats maintained that he was no longer in Croatia (*The Guardian* 29.09.03). But no one will be lobbying for the Serbs.

The case of Gotovina is regrettably typical of some Croatian military leaders. His career was summarised in a full-page article in *Le Monde* (February 4, 2004, page 17). From the French Foreign Legion he became involved with a band of ultra right wing thugs and criminals operating on the French Riviera around Nice and Aix-en-Provence, who sometimes serve as bodyguards for Jean-Marie Le Pen. In 1986, he was sentenced in Paris to five years for a jewel robbery but got out the next year. After that his frequent trips to South America were believed by the French police to be related to drug trafficking. He is understood by French Internal Security now to carry a French passport and to have found refuge in south-east France thanks to the network of earlier contacts from the French Foreign Legion and from the extreme right in that region. It is unlikely that the ICTY prosecution will push too hard for his appearance before the Tribunal because he would not hesitate to tell the court that his 'Operation Storm' to drive the Serbs out of the Krajina had the support of the United States.

It is more than lobbying and protection like this that the Croats enjoy. According to Diana Johnstone they have at their service the most effective public relations operated in the United States by Ruder Finn Global Public Affairs. When thousands of Serbs were forced to flee from Croatia over the Sava river in May of 1994, with many women and children failing to make it, British and French representatives on the Security Council pressed for sanctions to be applied to Croatia as well as those already applied to Serbia. This was repeatedly blocked by Mrs Albright, then the US representative at the United Nations – a point emphasised by Milosevic in his defence (page 10236). Ruder Finn's chief Balkan operator claimed his proudest moment was in winning over Jewish opinion in the United States with his stories, in 1992, of 'ethnic cleansing' by the Serbs in Bosnia and of Serb operated 'death camps' – just like the Nazis.

In the autumn of that year, the International Red Cross reported 2,692 civilians held in temporary detention centres in Bosnia – 1,203 held in eight camps by Bosnian Serbs, 1,061 by Muslim forces in 12 camps, and 428 held by Croats in five camps. The 'mistake' which the Bosnian Serbs made, led by Radovan Karadzic, was to invite the world press to visit the Serb run camps, and take photographs. For Ruder Finn could then use these, including the famous picture of the 'thin man behind the barbed wire' at Omarska. It only became clear later that this man and those with him were in fact outside the barbed wire, but the photograph could be used to suggest to the world that the Serbs ran camps like the Nazi concentration camps. The Yugoslav wars have been all along as much propaganda wars as military struggles.

That is not to deny that Serb forces committed some terrible acts in Bosnia, which have led the Tribunal to pronounce sentences of life imprisonment on some who have been tried in the Tribunal's other courts at The Hague, besides the chief court where Milosevic has appeared – the sentence of life imprisonment, for example, on Dr. Milomir Stakic, the doctor at Omarska. What is unacceptable is that these sentences should be passed on the decision of two out of three judges with no jury, and frequently on the basis of evidence much of which is hearsay. It is only right, moreover, that this should be set in the context of reports of similar horrors which have been perpetrated on the other side. Milosevic is adept at pointing this out. When he was questioning a witness from the Bosnian Association of Detainees who claimed that 200,000 non-Serbs had been held in Serb camps (page 17429), he discovered from her that she herself had been held in a Croatian run camp.

Milosevic shows himself to be a smart and indefatigable lawyer, despite his ill health which has occasionally interrupted the trial proceedings for a number of weeks at a time. The techniques he adopts for cross-examination have been to discredit the good faith of the more important non-Yugoslav witnesses, to quote other western sources expressing alternative views, and to question the veracity of local Albanian, Croat and Bosnian Muslim witnesses. Thus he was at pains to expose the previous associations of US Ambassador William Walker, who revealed the so-called 'massacre' at Racak, which became the pretext for the NATO bombing of Yugoslavia – Walker's connection with the Nicaraguan 'contras', his friendship with Madeline

Albright, and honorary membership of a US-Albanian Friendship Society. Milosevic, further, drew attention to the connections with British intelligence of Paddy Ashdown, who gave evidence of 'disproportionate' Serb military responses to KLA actions (page 2318). He questioned the close relationship of one of the peace negotiators at the Rambouillet conference, Ambassador Vollebaek, with Javier Solana, at that time NATO's Secretary-General (page 7239). He could also point to the pro-Albanian bias in a book written by Ambassador Petritsch, the chief negotiator at Rambouillet (page 7297).

Milosevic opened his defence against the charges relating to Croatia and Bosnia Hercegovina with a whole series of quotations from Western sources, exonerating him and accusing Croat and Muslim authorities of both blocking a peaceful settlement and carrying out deportations of Serb populations and burning of Serb villages as bad as anything of which the Serbs are accused. To answer the charge that the Serbs started it all, Milosevic was able to quote Cyrus Vance and David Owen, the chief UN negotiators in Bosnia: the first saying that it was 'premature German recognition of Slovenia and Croatia [by Europe and America] that led to the war'; the second saying that the 'United States… is responsible for the prolonged war in Bosnia' (pages 10273-4). Thorwald Stoltenberg, the other chief UN negotiator in Bosnia, is quoted (page 10312) saying on December 12, 1995 that 'President Slobodan Milosevic had played a key role in the peace process in Yugoslavia', the Serb side having in turn accepted all five peace proposals, which the others turned down.

In the matter of the expulsion of rival populations, Milosevic was able to quote Lord Carrington (page10254) giving a figure of '600,000 Serbs expelled from their territories in the then administered non-state borders of the republic of Croatia'. In the expulsion from Krajina of 200,000 Serbs by Croat forces in 'Operation Storm' of July 1995, thousands of whom died en route, US General Charles Boyd, deputy commander of NATO, was quoted by Milosevic, confirming that the US helped to plan and implement the attack (page 10241), and that 'what the Croatians called the 'occupied territories' is land that has been held by Serbs for more than three centuries' (page 10256).

When it came to comparing massacres on either side, Milosevic could give examples of the slaughter by Muslim forces of the Serb population of Bratunac on January 16, 1992, just three days after a peace plan had been agreed in Geneva. Milosevic was also able to quote the International Red Cross denying the huge numbers of executions of Muslims claimed to have taken place at the hands of Serb forces in Srebrenica. The history books now say 7,000 or 8,000 died, but the International Red Cross reported that many thousands turned up alive in Tuzla and Sarajevo (page 10260); and the Dutch blue helmets' report said that 'there is no indication that action was taken in collaboration with Belgrade' (page 10390). Zoran Ilic, Milosevic's predecessor as President of Yugoslavia, confirmed in his evidence at the Tribunal (page 22611) Milosevic's claim to have tried to dissuade the Serb commander Ratko Mladic from entering Srebrenica, which had been, although supposedly a safe haven, a Muslim base for raids on surrounding Serb villages. Ilic added that Milosevic was outraged at the massacre. But Ilic went on to say that he was surprised when Milosevic apparently supported the training of Serbian paramilitaries in Bosnia shortly before the Dayton Accords, when Bosnian Serbs were falling back in face of US armed Muslim and Croat forces.

Milosevic then drew a rather telling conclusion from all the evidence being brought to bear:

> 'The victims and casualties of the war against Yugoslavia were the innocent people from all three nations, all three ethnic groups. They were pushed into these conflicts because of foreign interests, other peoples' interests, but along with the full co-operation of their mindless leaders who led them to their deaths.' (page 19279)

If this conclusion is correct, and I believe that it is, then two questions have to be asked: first, why the international community, that is to say the leaders of the United States and the European Union, ganged up against Milosevic and the Serbs; and, secondly, why world opinion went along with them. The answer to the first question will only become clear from an understanding of the whole story of the rivalry of the United States, Germany, France and Russia for hegemonic power in Europe. The second question can only be answered by asking why journalists and others on the spot almost unanimously took the side of the Croats and Muslims and later the Kosovars against the Serbs. One reason has already been suggested, that most journalists and other foreign correspondents would arrive in Yugoslavia with no previous knowledge of the country, would be looking for a good story and would listen to whoever had the most effective public relations, and this would always be the Croats with the backing of the United States and Germany.

In Sarajevo, moreover, Muslim forces drove the journalists out of the first hotel they were based in, at Ilidza outside Sarajevo. When they were not in Zagreb, they settled in the Holiday Inn, situated in the central Muslim part of Sarajevo, under bombardment by Serb guns. The Moslems became the poor victims, and were not above firing on their own people and blaming the Serbs in order to win world support. On top of this the story of Sarajevo as a multicultural city, which it had once been, was given heroic status like the republican forces in the Spanish civil war. The Serbs were portrayed by influential writers such as David Rieff, in his book *Slaughterhouse* (Vintage 1998), and by his mother Susan Sontag, as seeking to destroy the city's multicultural nature. In fact, Sarajevo's famous newspaper, *Oslobodzenja*, continued to refuse to take sides. The true situation can only be understood by looking at the whole history of Former Yugoslavia, which requires a whole book to attempt. A brief summary will be given here.

German and American Interests

Milosevic, in his summing up of the civil war, which was quoted above, blamed 'foreign interests, other peoples' interests' for pushing the Yugoslav peoples into war; and we have seen that two of the chief UN peace negotiators, Cyrus Vance and David Owen, took the same view. We have to ask why they should have done that and why, in particular, the Americans and the Germans should have taken against the Serbs so strongly in a civil war in Yugoslavia – the Germans supporting the Croats and the Americans the Muslims. We have already noticed Klaus Kinkel calling for a tribunal to prosecute Serbs for their crimes. Kinkel had followed Hans-Dietrich Genscher as Germany's Foreign Minister, as a Free Democrat partner in Chancellor Kohl's government. The US negotiator for the UN in Bosnia, Cyrus Vance, referred to the Bosnian war as 'Genscher's war'.

Klaus Kinkel is reported by his biographer as having said only a week after taking office in May of 1992, 'We must force Serbia to its knees.' Kinkel had in the 1980s been head of the German intelligence service (the BND), which, I knew, had long-standing links with the diaspora of the Croat *Ustashe*, who had fought on the side of the Germans in the Second World War.

Germany was the chief instigator of the European recognition of the independence of Slovenia and Croatia from the former Yugoslavia, when Chancellor Kohl persuaded Britain's Prime Minister, John Major, to fall into line, offering Britain in exchange exemption from the Maastricht Treaty social clauses and from adoption of the Euro. Announcing the reunification of Germany, Chancellor Kohl, as Diana Johnstone reports, had made a solemn promise:

> 'With its national unity restored, our country will serve peace in the world. In the future Germany will send only peace into the world. We are well aware that the inviolability of borders and the respect for the territorial integrity and the sovereignty of all states in Europe is a basic condition for peace.' 'But', he added, 'at the same time, we stand by the moral and legal obligations resulting from history.'

Recognition of Croatia made Serbia an aggressor, and justified German arms being supplied in defence of Croatia's territorial integrity, while the 'obligations resulting from history' permitted the sending of German troops outside of Germany to take part in the policing of Bosnia and sending arms to the 'Liberation Army' in Kosovo.

Chancellor Kohl's government was replaced in 1998 by a Social Democratic-Green coalition. What was their interest in destabilising Serbia? The same restraints on German military actions outside Germany remained, and were even strengthened by the pacifist convictions of many German 'Greens'. Their leader, Joschka Fischer, who became Germany's Foreign Secretary, had to retain the support of his less pragmatic, less 'realist' Green comrades. It was the peace movement in Germany, especially among the young after 1968, that made it possible for Europe to accept German reunification in 1990. It was Joschka Fischer's pacifist associations, despite his street-fighting past, that made possible the bridging of the dilemma for Germany between sending 'only peace in the world' and the 'obligations of German history'. Thus, in Diana Johnstone's view, were laid the foundations for what came to be called 'humanitarian intervention'.

The concept of 'humanitarian intervention', which became the chief justification used by apologists for America's wars – those like Michael Ignatieff in *Warriors' Honour* (Chatto &Windus 1998) and Mary Kaldor in *One Year After Dayton, Dayton Continued*, (Helsinki Citizens Assembly) – had a somewhat earlier history according to Diana Johnstone. It went back to a 1992 study by the Carnegie Foundation under the presidency of Morton Abramowitz, who became an advisor to the Kosovo Albanian delegation at the Rambouillet peace conference in 1999 and champion of the Kosovo Liberation Army. His group of specialists in the early 1990s included US Secretary of State Madeline Albright and US Ambassador Richard Holbrooke, the US negotiator with Milosevic over the Kosovo question. Johnstone regards this group as not so much a conspiracy than a small elite group who took it upon themselves to decide how the immense power of the United States was to be used. Madeline Albright is said to have asked Colin Powell, when he was chief of the US military staff, 'What was the use of having this wonderful army you are always boasting about if we never use it?' The fact was that the military industrial complex of the United States needed the army to be used to sustain demand for their products. Their factories and their investments were the dynamo of the American economy. But why Yugoslavia when there are so many other places where the United States could, and did, deploy its armed forces?

One answer was given by Susan Woodward in her 1995 book *Balkan Tragedy*, and has been endorsed subsequently by Peter Gowan in *The Twisted Road to Kosovo* (Labour Focus on Eastern Europe, 1999). It goes like this. The collapse of the Soviet Union not only left NATO and its large US component without an obvious purpose, but left the whole of Europe open to the major Western European powers to unite and extend their influence eastwards, without the need for American support. Such a development would not at all have been in the interest of the United States, which proceeded to do all in its power to prevent it. NATO had to become more of an instrument for subordinating European ambitions to American interests. The combined European military force – Eurocorps – proposed in 1991 by the German and French governments, had to be brought under NATO and therefore under US command. Expansion eastwards had to take place as part of NATO in a 'Partnership for Peace', and should be extended to the Ukraine. Russia under Yeltsin was to be attracted into an American, not a European, economic and political embrace.

All these moves needed to be hardened up to serve American interests, so the argument continues. Germany after the two halves were re-united was a powerful force, conscious of what Chancellor Kohl had called 'the moral and legal obligations of history'. The German commitment to humanitarian intervention, then, was both economic and political. The Social Democrat Chancellor Schroeder, when he came to Kosovo to visit German troops at the end of NATO's war against Yugoslavia, was, he said, 'deeply moved in the context of German history in this region'. Since some of the Kosovars greeted him with the Nazi salute, Diana Johnstone wondered whether he was suffering from embarrassment, ignorance or amnesia. For some of those saluting will almost certainly have been sons or relatives, or even surviving members, of the SS Skanderbeg division recruited into Hitler's army, which had been responsible for mass murders of Serbs in Kosovo during the German occupation in 1941-5. There was no doubt, however, that Schroeder was taking seriously those 'obligations of history'.

What then are the 'obligations of German history'? They have to be concerned with the historic role of Germans, which include Austrians, in the defence of Europe, as their inheritance from the Holy Roman Empire. It has as ever to embrace the whole of Catholic Europe, including Franco-German solidarity, Poles, Slovaks and Hungarians, and of course Slovenes and Croats. But it stops at Russia and Serbia at the line drawn in AD 395 down the middle of modern Bosnia which divided the Western (Catholic) Empire from the Eastern (Orthodox) Empire. East of that line and south of the Danube are barbarians. The Greeks have to be allowed in, but this historic division between East and West, more than any anxiety about human rights, appears to be what keeps Serbs, and the Turks, out of the European Union.

The big question in 1991 for the future of Yugoslavia concerned the response of the United States to this new greater Germany. While

German involvement in the dissolution of Yugoslavia was evidently enthusiastic from the start, American involvement was at first hesitant. The US ambassador at Belgrade, Warren Zimmerman, had made it clear in January 1991 that Yugoslavia, having lost its special status as a bastion against the Soviet Bloc, President Milosevic could not expect any support for the use of force to disarm the Croat paramilitary forces so as to stop Croatia's secession from the federation. Thereafter the Americans seemed at first disposed to let Europe settle the Yugoslav question with the aid of the United Nations. But when fighting spread to Bosnia the US ambassador encouraged the Muslims, in March 1992, to renege on a UN peace plan, which had been negotiated for a tripartite solution within Yugoslavia, and hold out for a unitary independent Bosnian state under Moslem leadership. This new state would then have US support politically and militarily. Subsequent Peace Plans were all accepted by Milosevic, but not by the Croats or the Muslims. Had they been accepted, the horrors of the Bosnian war in 1993 and 1994 would have been avoided, but, from the American point of view, Germany and the European Union would have got the benefit of major influence in the region.

US influence in Yugoslavia was certainly greatly strengthened under the Clinton Presidency with the encouragement by the US of a Muslim-Croat federation to offset the Serbs in Bosnia-Hercegovina, followed by American armed support for a Croatian military action to drive all Serbs out of the Krajina in north western Bosnia. What changed US policy, according to Diana Johnstone, was that support for Bosnia's Muslim population and for the claim of the nationalist Bosnian Muslim leader Alija Izetbegovic for a Bosnian unitary state would serve to persuade Arab Islamic opinion in the Middle East that the USA did not only support Jews. The Gulf War had only recently been 'won' and US forces were firmly, if not so popularly, established on land in Saudi Arabia as well as in Kuwait and in the air above the no-fly zones to the north and south of Iraq. It was also hoped that it would help to cement the US alliance with Turkey. The newly elected US President Clinton delivered himself of a remarkable interpretation of world history to the effect that 'the Serbs had already started two world wars and should be prevented from starting a third'.

Susan Woodward and Peter Gowan would argue that the aim of establishing American supremacy over the expanding European Union was more important. The fact in any case was that by the mid-1990s the US military-industrial establishment was moving towards the view that the United Nations was an obstacle to the extension of US military interventions through NATO, where these were required to maintain the new US military's declared policy of 'full spectrum world dominance.' UN support had been won for the Gulf War because Saddam Hussein had manifestly aggressed against Kuwait. It might not always be so easy another time – as was proved in 2003 over war in Iraq. The UN's 'failure' in Yugoslavia could be used to demonstrate the absolute necessity for US action through NATO, which had to be beefed up to contain German ambitions after the collapse of the Soviet Union. Hence the involvement of the United States in the 1995 Dayton Accords, which ended the Bosnian war with a new state of Bosnia-Hercegovina shorn of the bits that Croatia annexed. These Accords were supposedly accepted by the Bosnian Serbs because of the entry of US planes to bomb the Serbian army HQ at Pale, but were perhaps more realistically explained by the invitation to the Yugoslav president Milosevic to underwrite the peace settlement. For this meant the ending of the damaging sanctions imposed on Serbia and the recognition of what was left of Former Yugoslavia.

Summing up the Case against Milosevic

It is impossible to come away from listening in to the Tribunal proceedings or reading the transcripts of the stories of hundreds of Bosnian Muslim and Albanian Kosovan witnesses without being convinced that terrible acts were performed in Bosnia by the Serbian armed forces, especially after the United States declared its support for the Muslims and Croats, and in Kosovo, especially after the NATO bombing began. Milosevic was able to make a good case for reprisals against the terrorist tactics of the Kosovo Liberation Army (KLA) before the NATO bombing, but once the bombing began he could not conceal the fact that the Serbs in Kosovo as in Bosnia responded to outside intervention with utter ruthlessness. It is not at all clear, however, that Milosevic was responsible or approved of the actions that Serb forces were involved in. Nor is there any evidence according to impartial investigators that the number of refugees or of cases of rape were, in fact, anywhere near the numbers reported, or that one should believe the wilder claims that acts of barbarism were committed. Milosevic was able to show in cases cited of so-called Serb barbarity, that decapitating of bodies and gouging out of eyes were the result in fighting of multiple bullet wounds to the neck after shoot-outs and of dogs and birds. scavenging among the corpses.

Milosevic was particularly sharp in cross-examining poor Albanian peasants who had been brought as witnesses to the Tribunal. They certainly appeared to have been put up to tell their stories, often obvious falsehoods. They were made to contradict themselves and to tell contrary stories and were asked by Milosevic again and again whether some incident had been seen by them personally or was something they had heard about from others. On several occasions the judges had to intervene to complain of hearsay evidence being presented to the court (e.g. page 7384). What was abundantly clear was the hatred these peasants expressed for the Serbs, but this had been inflamed by media excuses for outside support given to Albanian separatism. They had suffered in a war because they became involved in an armed revolt backed by outside forces.

The feelings of the Serbs towards the Germans and Americans who had intervened in their country are more difficult to define. Hundreds of thousands of Serb families are still refugees from their homes in Bosnia or in Kosovo, but this is not necessarily blamed on outside forces, however much the blame should in fact be placed there. A certain apathetic hopelessness has descended – in strong contrast to the firm wish to put the past behind them and start building a new future, which was the prevailing sense in 1945. Milosevic undoubtedly blames outside intervention for the worst horrors of the 1990s in his country. Milosevic's sharpest gibes were directed at one of the Prosecution's witnesses, the NATO chief of staff, General Klaus Naumann, concerning the political stance of the German government of Kohl and Genscher. It is impossible to read the transcript of the exchanges between Milosevic and Naumann without recognising Milosevic's ill concealed hatred of the man.

This led at one point to an extraordinary story told by Naumann

The Trial of Slobodan Milosevic

(page 6991) which he related as evidence of Milosevic's supposedly genocidal intentions in Kosovo. As Naumann reported the occasion, he and General Wesley Clark were discussing with Milosevic the increasingly unbalanced populations in Kosovo as a result of the higher birth rate of Albanians compared with Serbs. Milosevic was said to have hinted at a possible 'solution'. This was that 'we could do what we did at Drenica in '45 and '46.' And on being asked what that was, the answer apparently came, 'We got them together and shot them.'

On the face of it this was a truly dreadful remark, which deeply shocked Naumann and Clark. When Milosevic came to defend himself in cross examination with Naumann, he asked whether Naumann knew who these people were whom they rounded up at Drenica, and explained that they were marauding bands which had been recruited by the German army occupying Yugoslavia to do the dirty work of 'cleaning up' villages that were harbouring Partisans (page 7039). They were in fact rather more than that. They were what was left of the Albanians in the German army SS division, the Skanderbeg division. It was an utterly unacceptable suggestion from Milosevic as any sort of 'solution' for an imbalance in population, but it has to be understood in the light of the feelings about German generals that a patriotic Serb whose family had been active Partisans was bound to have.

It is not to say that one approves or condones such wartime atrocities. But it is not adequate evidence to convict Milosevic of war crimes that a Serb with strong Partisan connections like Milosevic can hardly forget, when talking to a German general about wars in Yugoslavia in the 1990s, that 50 years earlier several hundred thousand Serbs with Muslims, Jews and Romas were massacred by Croatian *Ustashe* allies of the German and Austrian forces, who were supervised in one notorious case by the man who became an Austrian President and General Secretary of the United Nations, Kurt Waldheim. On April 9th 1945 I was myself shown mass graves in Sarajevo of those who had been executed by the Germans as they retreated from the city four days before. The Serbs were perfectly capable of retaliating. The miracle was that Tito's Partisans successfully united the overwhelming majority of the Yugoslav peoples. Those who collaborated with the Germans escaped to form the diaspora with which Klaus Kinkel was working and which has been providing arms and propaganda for the new Croatian government, a government which once more flies the red and black checker board flag of the *Ustashe* that went into battle alongside the Nazi swastika against the Partisans in Yugoslavia.

One can hardly suppose that the judges at the Tribunal will take into account past sufferings of Serbs at the hands of the Germans and their allies in the Second World War, but they cannot avoid being influenced by the barrage of anti-Serb propaganda which preceded the trial of Milosevic and his fellow Serbians and which has not been stilled during its progress. This starts with the statement of charges. Quite different words are used in speaking of alleged crimes when they are applied to Serbs to those used to apply to Croats and Muslims. Only Serbs are said to have been involved in 'genocide'; the others committed 'war crimes'. Leading German government ministers have descended to racist language in speaking and writing about the Serbs as 'barbarians'. Milosevic is frequently likened to Hitler and the necessity of ending the Nazi regime cited as justification for bombing Yugoslavia.

The charge of genocide which is made against Milosevic and his associates requires that the prosecution proves a prior 'genocidal intent' in a 'joint criminal enterprise' to destroy an ethnic group in whole or in part. Much of the prosecution has therefore been concerned with Milosevic's reported statements, and with the direct connection between Milosevic as President of Yugoslavia and the army officers and paramilitary forces under his ultimate command. The case against Milosevic is that he openly advocated a single state for all Serbs, that as ultimate commander of the Yugoslav National Army (JNA) and police force (MUP), he retired senior officers who disagreed with him and replaced them with his friends, that he authorised the transfer of JNA arms and units to Serbian forces in Bosnia and to Serbian paramilitary groups, that he encouraged the criminal activities of these groups such as Arkan's 'red berets' and of so-called Serbian 'crisis staff' in driving non-Serbs out of their homes and villages in Bosnia-Hercegovina, that he knew about and did not stop maltreatment, including murder, of prisoners taken into Serbian concentration camps – all with the assumed aim of creating a wholly

Serbian occupied territory in Bosnia-Hercegovina which could be annexed to Serbia proper in a new Yugoslavia.

Milosevic's case has been that all Serbs in one state did not exclude other ethnic groups living in that state, as could be seen from the large numbers already living inside Serbia – of Hungarians in Vojvodina, and Muslims in the Sandjak (southern Serbia), to which many Muslims from Bosnia had fled; that the agreement reached between himself and Franjo Tudjman in 1991 for dividing up Bosnia-Hercegovina between Serbia and Croatia was designed to avoid war rather than to ignite it, and would indeed have averted war had it not been for the intervention of outside forces, mainly German and American, with their own agendas; that the retirement and replacement of JNA officers was a normal military process; that JNA arms were taken over by each of the Republics' Territorial Forces and the JNA was demobilised by Milosevic in May of 1992; that Milosevic repeatedly intervened in Bosnia to encourage Serbian forces to respect the laws of war (page 20233) and to discourage paramilitary activity (page 20244), and was frequently criticised by Bosnian Serb nationalists and by Serb nationalists in Serbia for not giving adequate support to the Serbs.

It is extremely unsatisfactory in a court of law, as the International Criminal Tribunal for Former Yugoslavia purports to be, that so much verbal evidence is taken, much of it based on hearsay with very little documentary evidence to back it up. Michael Scharf has calculated, according to Kirsten Sellars 'The Rise and Rise of Human Rights' (Sutton 2002), that as much as 90% of the evidence given at the trial has been based on hearsay. It has been particularly unsatisfactory that in the cases relating to Croatia and Bosnia, many witnesses for the prosecution have been heard and not seen in court, their identity being concealed and being referred to by a letter and a number. This has been the case with many of the Yugoslav officials and police and army officers who have been permitted to give their evidence *incognito*. Arguing the case for the defence in these circumstances becomes very difficult. It is also unsatisfactory that evidence is sometimes presented in the form of intercepted phonecalls, where the identity of the speaker has to be assumed to be what the prosecutor says it is and the circumstances likewise. An example of this occurs (on page 15921) when a voice which we are told is that of the indicted Bosnian Serb leader, Radovan Karadzic, appears to threaten that 'Sarajevo will be gone and 200,000 Muslims killed.'

Milosevic's case received some support from David Owen's statements in his book *Balkan Odyssey* (Indigo, London, 1996) that Milosevic did indeed support the various peace initiatives in Bosnia, but 'did not do enough', Owen says, despite being under the pressure of UN economic sanctions. It also received support from Zoran Ilic, one time President of the Serbian Party of Socialists (ex-Communists) and President of Yugoslavia after Milosevic's defeat in 2000. Ilic asserted that Milosevic was not responsible for the crime at Srebrenica, which remains the chief element in his indictment. Ilic insisted that Milosevic indeed sought to prevent the massacre (page 22611). It may be said that this was just a Serb supporting a Serb, but following after Milosevic one would expect that Ilic would be anxious to distance himself rather than give support.

Milosevic did not, by contrast, get support from Ante Markovic, a Croat and last Prime Minister of Former Yugoslavia, who accused him of using the JNA to prevent by force the dissolution of Yugoslavia (pages 28000 ff.) and of misappropriating funds to that end. Milosevic would not deny the accusation of using force to defend Yugoslavia. To do so was the duty of the JNA, which Milosevic pointed out (page 10219) was not dominated by Serbs at the top. The army chief Kadijevic was half Croatian, half Serb, the air force chief Jurijevic was Croatian, and the commander of the navy, Brovec, was a Slovene. Although in the end Serbs predominated in the JNA, Milosevic was right to point to the tradition in Tito's Yugoslavia of balancing ethnic backgrounds in official appointments. In any case, Markovic's accusations about the use of the JNA were rebutted by Borisav Jovic. He was a rotating Yugoslav President when the civil war broke out, who made it clear that Milosevic as President of Serbia at that time, and not then President of Yugoslavia, had no control over the JNA. Jovic also insisted that Milosovic did not have command responsibility for the Bosnian killings and had no plans for a 'Greater Serbia'.

The most damaging case against Milosevic made by Ante Markovic was that, while he did not regard Milosevic as a nationalist – rather, more interested in his own personal power (page 28042) – he did believe that Milosevic's aim was 'quite obvious: he was fighting for a greater Serbia'. However, in reading the transcripts, one has to remember that the prosecution was presenting Markovic's accusations against Milosevic – of giving orders to the army to defend the Krajina Serbs (page 23037), of taking Serbia's share of Yugoslavia's financial assets for his government (page 28012), and of ordering partial mobilisation (page 28064) – as if all these things were done before and not after Croatia moved to secede in June 1991, indeed over a year after the April 1990 elections in Croatia had given Tudjman a nationalist majority in the Croat Parliament determined on independence. Perhaps the most telling revelation in Markovic's statement was that Tudjman had made it clear to Markovic that the shelling of Dubrovnik and Vukovar by Serb/JNA forces 'suited him [Tudjman] in the sense of winning over arguments for his emancipation or for his secession and having Croatia recognised' (page 28039). Croatia and Slovenia were recognised by Germany in December 1991 and by the European Union and the United States in April 1992.

Markovic reported to the Tribunal (page 28026 ff.) the discussions he had with both Tudjman and Milosevic after their meeting in March 1991 at Karadjordjevo when the two of them agreed to divide up Bosnia-Hercegovina between Croatia and Serbia. Both replied to Markovic's fear that there would be appalling bloodshed if they did that, by saying that they did not expect it. Muslims, they said, whose families had once converted from Catholicism would join the Croats; those who had once converted from Orthodoxy would join the Serbs. Milosevic with greater realism had added that the Muslims would get an autonomous enclave to live in. Markovic said that he had responded to all this by insisting that he would oppose any such move with all the power at his command, which he admitted was by then very little. He had resigned by the end of the year. On being asked whether he had told Izetbegovic, the Muslim leader in Bosnia, of his intention to oppose the division of Bosnia-Hercegovina, Markovic said that he had done so – though not immediately. That was strange because Izetbegovic was then regularly giving Markovic copies of intercepts of messages between Milosevic and Karadzic, the Serb Bosnian leader, concerning the arming of Bosnian Serbs (page 28029).

The prosecution did not remind the Tribunal of it, but perhaps the judges will recall the fact that, by the time Milosevic was helping the Bosnian Serbs to arm, the Croats were receiving massive supplies of arms from Germany and elsewhere. Any justice that might come out of this trial will need to recognise that the tragedy of Yugoslavia cannot be blamed on one man or one side, but must involve condemnation of nationalists on all sides, and above all the complicity of the outside powers who were supporting them. What the trial cannot explain, by its very terms of reference, is how it came about that after nearly sixty years of extraordinarily successful development, Tito's Yugoslavia fell apart and ancient divisions between different faiths and nationalities were revived. To understand that we have to go back at least to the beginning of the Partisans' resistance to German occupation and to the German policy of dividing the Yugoslav peoples in order to conquer them. That understanding and recognition of the subsequent remarkable successes in reconciliation and rehabilitation achieved in Former Yugoslavia is the aim of my forthcoming book, *From Tito to Milosevic: Yugoslavia – The Lost Country* (see page 79).

A Study in Propaganda
Marlise Simons on the Yugoslavia Tribunal
Edward S. Herman and David Peterson

While the concept of a 'party line' is usually associated with totalitarian parties and their offshoots, controlled by a state that imposes a politically serviceable version of history on its underlings and agents, it is very common for something like a party line to emerge in the U.S. mainstream media as they deal with a demonised target accused of misbehaviour. In such cases the media quickly jump onto a bandwagon that takes the official and politically convenient view as obvious truth, and they then devote their efforts to elaborating on that truth.

This was the case in the years 1981-1986, following the shooting of Pope John Paul II in Rome in May 1981 by the rightwing Turk, Mehmet Ali Agca. These were years in which the Reagan administration was attempting to portray the Soviet Union as an 'evil empire,' and it welcomed anything helpful in Soviet denigration. It was soon charged in the *Readers' Digest,* NBC News, and elsewhere that the Bulgarians and KGB were behind the shooting, and this theme was latched onto and became a *de facto* party line with great speed. There was virtually complete closure on questions of the validity of the charge, and the media devoted all their efforts to filling in details and obtaining speculations on why the KGB did this and its political ramifications. The charge was in fact untrue, as came out in a Rome trial against the Bulgarians that ended in 1986, in CIA officer disclosures in 1990, and in the absence of any supportive evidence from the newly opened secret service files of the now allied Bulgaria. The mainstream media quietly crept away from the story in which their performance had been outlandish in terms of adherence to theoretical news values – with the *New York Times* among the most outlandish – but outstanding in terms of propaganda service to ongoing state policy.[1]

A very similar process can be seen in the media's treatment of the Balkan conflicts in the years 1990-2004. Here also a party line that conformed to the political aims of the governing elite gradually emerged and eventually hardened into unchallengeable truth. In a broad sketch of the official line – also the standard media version – there was a bad man, a Communist holdover and dictator, who used nationalist appeals to mobilise his people, who were 'willing executioners.'[2] This bad man strove for a 'Greater Serbia' and in the process committed major crimes of ethnic cleansing and genocide that were initiated and mainly carried out by him and his forces. The West, led by the United States, belatedly entered this fray, eventually bombing the bad man's proxy forces in Bosnia, forcing the Dayton Agreement on him, but with the West still eventually compelled to war against him to protect the Kosovo Albanians. The West organised a Tribunal in 1993 to deal with his and others' crimes, and that Tribunal, though hampered by sluggish cooperation from the West and more serious obstruction by the Serbs, has done yeoman service in the cause of justice and reconciliation.[3]

This party line, which is contestable on each facet of its claims,[4] entered into the premises of journalists and editors at the *New York Times*, just as the line on the Bulgarian-KGB link to the Papal shooting gripped them for many years (followed by silence, without apology), with closure imposed in both cases. The *Times* reporter who was most familiar with Yugoslavia, but who failed to adhere to the party line, David Binder, was removed from the region in favor of less knowledgeable but more accommodating journalists, just as Raymond Bonner was removed from reporting on Central America in the 1980s for his failure to adhere to the party line evolving there.[5]

We will illustrate this party line treatment in the Balkans wars by examining the work of Marlise Simons in her coverage of the International Criminal Tribunal for the Former Yugoslavia (ICTY, or simply Tribunal) for the *New York Times*. Simons has been the paper's principal reporter on the Tribunal and one of the paper's leading reporters on the Balkans in general, and as we would expect, and as we will show, she has been an undeviating adherent to the party line. Our analysis is based on the study of her entire output of 120 articles dealing with the Tribunal, extending from December 7, 1994 to December 14, 2003 (excluding only her articles with fewer than 200 words).[6]

Sourcing

A party line commonly takes its cues and information from official sources.

A Study in Propaganda

The accompanying table shows how much Marlise Simons has depended on Tribunal and NATO officials for her information and as a guide to what was relevant (rows 1-6). These account for almost half of her sources (48.6 percent); and if we include the human rights group officials cited by Simons, all of whom were entirely sympathetic with the Tribunal's work,[7] and indictees who had agreed to plead guilty and cooperate with the Tribunal, we are over half (53.8 percent). If we remove the category 'other,' most of whose members were supportive of the Tribunal, the ratio rises to 60.1 percent. Virtually all of the sources cited by Simons that contest the party line are indictees and defence counsel (lines 8B and 9). She cites only a single witness for the defence, as compared with 32 witnesses for the prosecution and four prosecution experts.

TABLE 1
Sources used by Marlise Simons in reporting on the Tribunal[8]

Sources	Number of Articles	Percent of Articles	Percent of Total Less 'Other'
1. ICTY Personnel:	125	30.9	34.9
2. Prosecution Witnesses:	32	7.9	8.9
3. Prosecution Experts:	4	1.0	1.1
4. Indictments:	11	2.7	3.1
5. ICTY Court Judgments:	7	1.7	2.0
6. NATO Country Officials:	19	4.7	5.3
7. Human Rights Group Officials:	14	3.4	3.9
8. Indictees:	41	10.1	11.5
A) Class A:	6	1.4	1.7
B) Class B:	35	8.6	9.8
B-1 Milosevic alone:	26	6.4	7.3
9. Defense Counsel:	37	9.1	10.3
10: Defense Witnesses:	1	0.2	0.3
11. Defense Experts:	0	–	–
12. Experts With Dissident Views	0	–	–
13. Other:	49	12.0	13.7
* Totals:	407	100-	100-
** Totals minus 'other'	358		
*** Tabulations of interest:		Percentages of totals	
A: 1-6	198	48.6	55.3
B. 7 + 8A	20	4.9	5.6
C. A +B – 8A	218	53.6	60.1
D. 8B + 9 and 10	73	17.9	20.4
E. D – Milosevic	47	11.5	13.1

These numbers understate the bias, because the prosecution is given more prominence, more space, and more friendly treatment. Indictee and defence counsel statements are briefer, more often paraphrased, come deeper in the articles, and often give the appearance of a token inclusion designed to provide a nominal balance. Their words are sometimes in satire-intended quote marks highlighting their implausibility; and they are imbedded in articles in which Simons' sympathy and identification with the prosecution is readily apparent. (See **Language and Tone**, below.)

The most telling evidence of Simons' overwhelming bias in sourcing is the fact that in 120 articles she never cites a single independent expert who might have raised questions about the Tribunal's purpose, methods, or evidence. Among the informed critics ignored were: Charles Boyd, David Chandler, Phillip Corwin, Tiphaine Dickson, Fiona Fox, Robert Hayden, Jon Holbrook, Diana Johnstone, George Kenney, Raymond Kent, Hans Koechler, John Laughland, Michael Mandel, General Lewis Mackenzie, General Satish Nambiar, Jan Oberg, Walter Rockler, Alfred Rubin, Kirsten Sellars and Cedric Thornberry. One of these excluded experts, Robert Hayden, actually gave lengthy testimony during the Tribunal hearings on the case of Dusko Tadic on September 10-11, 1996. Hayden was contesting the views of James Gow, a prosecution witness. Simons cited at length Gow's testimony for the prosecution, and noted that Gow provided the courtroom a 'history lesson' in the wars that consumed Yugoslavia, portraying these wars as the result of a 'plan conceived in Belgrade.' But Simons never cited Hayden's testimony for the defense.[9] We see here in miniature a pattern that has repeated itself throughout not only Marlise Simons' reporting on the affairs of the Tribunal for the *Times* – but throughout the *Times* coverage of the breakup of Yugoslavia overall.

Framing

Framing and sourcing are closely linked, as the use of a particular source allows that source to define the issues and to fix the frames of reference, presumably those acceptable to or preferred by the journalist. Thus in the case of the Papal assassination attempt of 1981, the Italian government and prosecutors took as their frame the certainty that the KGB and Bulgarians had hired Agca to shoot the Pope – and after 17 months in an Italian prison, and numerous indications by his interrogators that they would be pleased to find a KGB-Bulgarian connection, along with a variety of inducements, Agca, while also periodically claiming to be Jesus Christ, had 'confessed' to the connection. The U.S. media took this as a truth around which the story was framed. Similarly, in Moscow in 1936, the prosecutor's claim that Leon Trotsky had organised a conspiracy to overthrow the Soviet government, supported by documents and confessions, was the frame used by the Soviet media as well as the prosecutor. In each of these cases there were alternative frames, but the media ignored them.

The frame within which the Tribunal worked was in effect a morality tale, with a clear cut delineation of good and bad players, as described in the third paragraph above. As regards the Tribunal itself, in the Tribunal, NATO official, and establishment media frame (which are identical) the Tribunal was obviously good – independent, without political bias and simply seeking justice, adhering to Western judicial standards, and working under difficult conditions because of imperfect cooperation from the West and more severe obstructionism from Yugoslavia. This was Marlise Simons' frame and she never once departed from or questioned it. She repeatedly made contestable assertions about recent Balkan history as unarguable truths, such as that Milosevic was 'the man whom the world has seen stoke a decade of war and bloodshed in the Balkans,' a claim that she usually offers in the form of the charges by the prosecution – 'chief architect,' 'most responsible' – a simple-minded view that Lenard Cohen has described as the 'paradise lost/loathsome leaders' perspective.[10] Not once in 120 articles does Simons provide an analysis or discussion of the litany of prosecution charges and party line claims about the Balkan wars that she regurgitates like a press officer of the Tribunal. For Simons the Tribunal is the agent of justice in the morality tale, so that she accepts its claims as assuredly true and its self-appraisal as independent and virtuous and feels no obligation to ask any hard questions or probe into areas that might suggest doubts about its role or methods.

There were alternative frames, however, among which we may distinguish: (1) the Tribunal as a planned and effective political and public relations arm of NATO; and (2) the Tribunal as a 'rogue court,' without legal standing, that has violated numerous Western judicial principles in its eagerness to achieve its assigned political goals. These alternative frames have been employed by most of the 20 independent experts named above, so that their exclusion was obviously linked to the fact that the alternative frames were unwelcome to Simons and the *New York Times*. The alternative frames were allowed only in statements by Slobodan Milosevic, who did denounce his incarceration and trial, and the work of the Tribunal in general, as strictly and unjustly political. This is a fine illustration of a standard ploy in propaganda service: confine the unwanted line of argument to the mouth of somebody who has little credibility with the target audience, making it easy to dismiss without confronting serious argument and facts.

With the prosecution as her guide and almost exclusive source of information, Simons' articles largely repeat prosecution charges, transmit the gist of evidence of the scores of witnesses produced by the prosecution, and absent any critical and independent counter-evidence and analyses, confirm and reinforce the prosecution case, and public acceptance of the morality tale. This replicates the performance of the *New York Times* in the case of the attempted Papal assassination, where the reporters' tacit assumption of the truth of the Bulgarian-KGB involvement, 'news' featuring confidently stated official claims and purported corroborating evidence – e.g., 'we have the evidence that Agca worked in close collaboration with the Bulgarians;' and 'all the evidence suggests'[11] – and blacking out of inconvenient facts and dissident analysis, strengthened common belief in the 'Bulgarian connection.'

In her reporting on the Tribunal, Simons repeatedly refers to prosecution 'momentum,' confidence and exhilaration, claims that they have 'solid' evidence, with hints that if they don't have enough it is because of effective cover-up by the bad man.[12] Scores of times she mentions the numbers allegedly killed in Bosnia and at Srebrenica, and charges of Milosevic's and Serb responsibility, with conflicting evidence, context that brings in the shared NATO-power and Bosnian Muslim and Croatian responsibility for the violence, and alternative analyses, blacked out.[13] She reports in detail numerous witness accounts of alleged violence suffered at the hands of the Serb army and paramilitaries, extracting maximum emotional leverage from these testimonials.[14]

Apart from her uncritical treatment of these witness accounts, Simons never once suggests that this kind of mistreatment of civilians occurs in every civil conflict and war, and that the Serbs could produce a very large number of civilian witnesses to similar abuses inflicted on them by Bosnian Muslims, Croats, and the U.S. Air Force.[15] Early in his trial Milosevic spent two days showing slides that gave graphic detail on numerous civilian victims of the U.S. bombing of Serbia, and he suggested that a formidable case could be built against the United States and NATO by a Tribunal that had different political ends. Simons mentioned his evidence briefly, but she did not pause to reflect on his case or bring in an expert who might expand on it.[16] When the issue of NATO culpability in its deliberate bombing of civilian facilities came up during and after the 78-day bombing, Simons and her paper evaded the issue and provided only NATO-Tribunal apologetics, as described below.

Language and Tone

Marlise Simons' language and tone clearly reflected her belief that the Yugoslavia conflict was a simple case involving 'loathsome leaders' and their victims, now seeking justice, with NATO and the Tribunal the forces for justice. In this frame, the Tribunal, its prosecutors and judges, and its NATO supporters were good; Milosevic and his associates and Bosnian Serb leaders were evil. With this 'journalism of attachment'[17] the use of neutral or positive language – 'purr words' – in describing the good people, and negative language – 'snarl words' – in describing the villains comes easily and appears completely natural to the biased journalist. Conflicts between Good and Evil seem entirely obvious; and editors similarly biased do not complain.

The result can be childish and comical in the implausible manner in which the villains are regularly derogated and the heroes lauded. *Table 2* illustrates this with a comparison of Simons' language used to describe Milosevic, on the one hand, and the two prosecutors, Louise Arbour and Carla Del Ponte, and Judge Richard May, on the other hand. This tabulation is not biased, as Simons uses *no* positive language for Milosevic and *no* negative language in reference to Arbour, Del Ponte and May in any of the 120 sample articles. The negative language Simons used as regards Milosevic is far from exhausted with the items included in this table.

TABLE 2
Marlise Simons' word usage

Slobodan Milosevic	Prosecutors Louise Arbour and Carla Del Ponte; Judge Richard May
Infamous	Forceful (Arbour)
Sniped	Resolute (Arbour)
Scoffed	New assertiveness (Arbour)
Smirk on his face	Very capable (Arbour)
Speechmaking	No-nonsense style (Arbour)
Badgers the simple conscripts	Tough crime fighter (Del Ponte)
Carping	Unswerving prosecutor (Del Ponte)
Blustery defense	Natural fighter (Del Ponte)
Loud and aggressive	Unrelenting hunter (Del Ponte)
Notorious	Finding the truth (Del Ponte)
Defiant	Keeping tight control (May)
Reverted to sarcasm	Patiently repeated questions (May)
Contemptuous	Sober, polite and tough (May)
Outbursts	Expert on evidence (May)
Face often distorted with anger	Among the best suited (May)

This differential usage cannot be explained on the grounds that Arbour, but not Milosevic, was 'resolute' and 'forceful,' and that May was only 'sober, polite and tough,' whereas Milosevic was 'contemptuous' and 'carping.' Milosevic was frequently as resolute and forceful as Arbour, but Simons reserves such positive language for people she approves and always finds Milosevic to be defiant, loud, aggressive, and blustering. The noted Toronto lawyer Edward L. Greenspan, attending the opening of the Milosevic trial, was immediately impressed with the fact that May 'clearly reviles Milosevic' and that he 'doesn't even feign impartiality, or indeed, interest.'[18] But Simons would never call this attitude, so obvious to Greenspan, 'contemptuous.' Numerous trial observers have noted how May continuously interferes with Milosevic's cross-examinations in a manner that could reasonably be called 'carping' or far worse, as we discuss below. Simons reserves such a word for the bad man.

Simons several times describes Carla Del Ponte interacting with one of her allies in the court room at something Milosevic says – 'Del Ponte...occasionally shot a smile at other prosecutors in apparent incredulity'[19] – a journalistic device reinforcing the overall tone of good and reasonable on the prosecution's side and evil and foolishness on the side of the defendant. As we will also see below, 'unrelenting hunter' Carla Del Ponte turned somersaults of evasion to deny petitions to pursue an investigation of possible war crimes by NATO – she has been 'relentless' only in pursuing NATO-approved villains. But when Simons interviewed Del Ponte and described her as the 'unrelenting hunter,' she failed to ask Del Ponte about the Tribunal's deflection of charges against NATO – and in fact, in the 120 articles that comprise this study, Simons never asked any Tribunal official a challenging question or raised one for somebody else to answer. In short, Simons has been on the Tribunal-NATO 'team' from the start of her coverage of its work in late 1994, reflected in sourcing, framing, word usage, and tone. The result has been deeply corrupt journalism that is *de facto* propaganda service.

The Neglected Political Model: The Tribunal as the Pseudo-Judicial Public Relations Arm of NATO

By avoiding the alternative frames, Marlise Simons has been able to bypass or deflect inconvenient facts that interfered with her morality tale and that would put the Tribunal's work in a less favourable light. Let us take a closer look at each of the alternative frames, and see how Simons dealt with some of the facts that lend those frames salience.

The first alternative frame – the Tribunal as the pseudo-judicial public relations arm of NATO – rests on structural facts, admissions by some of the principals, and, most importantly, on the Tribunal's performance record. The Tribunal was a creation of the U.N. Security Council,[20] with the United States, Britain and Germany playing lead roles, the United States most prominently and increasingly so. It is of interest that the United States has refused any cooperation with the new International Criminal Court because of the alleged threat that charges might be levelled against U.S. citizens based on a 'politically motivated' ICC agenda.[21] The United States has never feared this of the ICTY, however, because of the crucial U.S. role in organising the Tribunal, financing it (along with other close NATO allies), staffing it, vetting its judges and prosecutors, supplying it with its police force, providing it with information, and giving it political support.

During the 78-day bombing war, when moves were made by dissident legal experts and others to persuade the Tribunal to investigate the NATO leadership for crimes related to their war, NATO public relations spokesman Jamie Shea responded to a question on the Tribunal's jurisdiction over NATO's conduct as follows:

> I believe that when Justice Arbour starts her investigation, she will because we will allow her to....NATO are the people who have been detaining indicted war criminals for the Tribunal in Bosnia...NATO countries are those that have provided the finance to set up the Tribunal, we are amongst the majority financiers...we want to see war criminals brought to justice and I am certain that when Justice Arbour goes to Kosovo and looks at the facts she will be indicting people of Yugoslavia nationality and I don't anticipate any others at this stage.[22]

Neither Marlise Simons nor any other *New York Times* reporter has ever quoted Shea's statement, which suggests NATO control of the Tribunal – that 'he who pays the piper calls the tune' (Kirsten Sellars)[23] – and which Shea indicates will surely exempt NATO officials from prosecution, as in fact it did. Nor have Simons or her *Times* colleagues ever mentioned the hyperlink to the NATO web site conveniently placed on the ICTY home page throughout the period when it was supposedly considering a petition charging NATO with war crimes.[24] It should be noted that the Tribunal's mandate does not limit its reach to Yugoslavs for prosecution for war crimes in Yugoslavia, a point never discussed by Simons (or other *Times* reporters). Evasions such as this have been helped along by ignoring statements like Shea's.

Simons also has never discussed the U.S.-dominant staffing and vetting of Tribunal staff, and she has never mentioned the May 9, 1996 NATO-Tribunal 'memo of understanding' that gave NATO the task of serving as the Tribunal's police force. She has acknowledged U.S. funding only in passing, without addressing its possible impact on Tribunal policy. Article 16 of the Tribunal's charter states that the prosecutor shall act independently and shall not seek or receive instruction from any government. But can the prosecutor act independently if dependent on specific governments for funding,

A Study in Propaganda

personnel, information, and police service? Simons never raises the question. Even within the establishment it is sometimes acknowledged that the Tribunal was organised to serve NATO political aims. As Michael Scharf, the man who wrote the Tribunal's charter for Secretary of State Madeleine Albright, once explained, the Tribunal was 'widely perceived within the government as little more than a public relations device and...useful policy tool....Indictments...would serve to isolate offending leaders diplomatically...and fortify the international political will to employ economic sanctions or use force.'[25]

There have been other statements by Western officials that imply that the Tribunal will do what they want it to do. Thus, the *New York Times* reported in July, 1999 that 'Washington has threatened Mr. Draskovic with indictment by the international war crimes tribunal in the Hague for the activities of his short-lived Serbian Guard, a paramilitary group, in Croatia in 1991.'[26] A U.S. government fact sheet stated that 'We will make a decision on whether Yugoslav actions against ethnic Albanians constitute genocide...The ICTY will indict those responsible for crimes against humanity and genocide.' British officials have also made similar statements implying they possess the power to bring the Tribunal into action.[27]

Simons gets around the structural and other evidence of the external control and associated political bias of the Tribunal by confining the discussion of this issue to Tribunal prosecutors. Her complete exclusion of dissident experts is important here – most of these experts have featured the Tribunal as a 'political court' (Edward Greenspan) and 'means of effecting policy' (Christopher Black), an 'instrument of revenge rather than justice' (Jon Holbrook) whose indictments are of a 'purely political nature' (Hans Koechler), at once the 'judicial arm of NATO' (Kirsten Sellars) and the 'propaganda arm of NATO' too (Michael Mandel), politics flowing from the purpose, organisation, funding and staffing of the Tribunal. Not surprisingly, the Tribunal prosecutors claim to be completely independent, with no agenda but pure justice, and they complain about how hard it is to get cooperation from their organisers, funders, information- and staff-providers, and police agents in their unbiased search for justice.[28] It never occurs to Simons that this claim of foot-dragging might be a self-serving and disingenuous effort to obscure the high degree of Tribunal dependence and *de facto* agency function, a claim and effort advantageous to both the International Criminal Tribunal for Former Yugoslavia and its principals. She has never discussed the difference between the U.S. treatment of the Tribunal and the International Criminal Court, which suggests an inordinate U.S. fear of judicial independence and would raise questions about Tribunal independence that Simons steadily evades. For Simons and the *New York Times*, the official view simply is the truth and enters the 'news' as such. Thus, in a summary on the 'Tribunal: How It Works,' the paper affirmed that 'The Office of the Prosecutor operates independently of the Security Council, of any state or international organisation and of other organs of the Tribunal.'[29] And that was the end of it. The Tribunal's truth is the whole truth, and nothing but the truth.

Perhaps even more important, Simons avoids mention or the slightest hint of critical analysis of the many manifestations of political service rendered to NATO by the Tribunal. As early as June, 1998, NATO began planning for its springtime 1999 war over Kosovo to coincide with the Alliance's 50th Anniversary celebration, scheduled to be held in Washington, D.C., in April, 1999. Almost immediately, the Tribunal followed in NATO's wake with an intensified focus on the Serbs, and a steady stream of press releases on Serb conduct in the province. Thus, for example, Marlise Simons reported in August 1998 that 'The United Nations war crimes tribunal is stepping up its investigations of war crimes in the Serbian province of Kosovo,' notwithstanding 'Serbian claims that events in the province...are an internal affair.'[30] The propaganda barrage escalated immediately following the claim of a Serb massacre in the ethnic Albanian village of Racak in January 1999, an incident which Arbour declared, on the basis of unverified information supplied her by U.S. official William Walker, was 'a massacre of civilians,' one that therefore 'falls squarely within the mandate of the ICTY'[31]; Arbour also generated considerable publicity by rushing to the scene of the alleged crime with Western cameramen in tow. This massacre claim was welcomed by U.S. officials, providing them with the eagerly sought pretext for the bombing war. When the U.S. Secretary of State Madeleine Albright first learned of Walker's allegations about the Racak incident, the *Washington Post* reported, she phoned National Security Adviser Sandy Berger. 'Spring has come early to Kosovo,' she told him.[32] Arbour's performance here was in serious violation of prosecutorial ethics, and her own claim that 'we certainly will not be advancing a case against anybody on the basis of unsubstantiated, unverifiable, *uncorroborated* allegation'[33], but it was beautifully geared to NATO propaganda service.

The same was true two months later, when Arbour announced an indictment of Serb paramilitary leader Zeljko Raznjatovic (Arkan), prepared in September, 1997, but not released until March 31, 1999, one week after the beginning of NATO's bombing war, and giving the war a further propaganda boost. Arbour's alleged reason for releasing this information at this particular time was that she wanted to put on notice anyone who 'might retain his [Arkan's] services or obey his orders,' and who 'will be tainted by their association with an indicted war criminal.'[34]

Then in April, as described by Kirsten Sellars, 'midway through the Kosovo conflict, Arbour made a whistle-stop tour of NATO capitals, collecting promises of assistance wherever she went.' Her trip to London 'seemed to be expressly designed to highlight the tribunal's support for one side of the war. She joined Robin Cook and chief of staff General Sir Charles Guthrie at a press conference held at the Ministry of Defence, the department responsible for Britain's attacks on Serbia.' At this press conference Arbour was publicly promised a major release of British intelligence material featuring alleged Serb atrocities. 'Answering a question put to her at the press conference, Louise Arbour stated that it was "inconceivable" that the tribunal was "servicing a political agenda." Yet her presence at this publicity stunt, designed to add to the swelling tide of atrocity stories already doing the rounds in the British media, belied her words.'[35] Marcus McGee, writing in the Toronto *Globe and Mail*, pointed out that 'It is part of NATO's war strategy to portray the leaders of Yugoslavia as war criminals who must be stopped. By accepting the documents, critics say, Judge Arbour risked becoming part of that strategy and losing her impartiality.'[36]

But Arbour's maximal performance as a NATO public relations agent took place in the midst of the bombing war, on May 22, 1999, when NATO, in order to hasten a Yugoslav surrender, began to bomb Serb civilian facilities, including bridges, factories, electric power and water facilities, and even schools and hospitals. This elicited growing criticism even in the NATO countries. At that juncture, Arbour rushed into action with an indictment of Milosevic (as well as four of his closest aides) for crimes against humanity and violations of the laws or customs of war, all based, once again, on unverified information provided her by U.S. and British officials. U.S. Secretary of State Albright and State Department public relations boss James Rubin quickly cited this latest indictment as a justification for the bombing campaign[37] – an example of the Tribunal's propaganda service that was not only crude, but in defence of NATO actions which themselves were clearly war crimes.[38]

At the same time that U.S. Government officials were citing the Tribunal's indictment of Milosevic as evidence of the justness of NATO's war, Arbour herself was explaining that, while individuals are 'entitled to the presumption of innocence until convicted,' the indictments of the Serb leadership 'raise serious questions about their suitability to be guarantors of any deal, let alone a peace agreement.'[39] In addition to contradicting herself by undertaking an action that presumed guilt, based on information as yet unverified by the Tribunal, Arbour took on the role of 'surrogate politician,' in Hans Koechler's words, announcing her personal political determination that Milosevic was to be ruled out as a negotiator.[40] On many other occasions, indictments were used by the Tribunal to criminalise and effectively remove individuals from the negotiating process. Milosevic had to depend on the Russians to negotiate on Yugoslavia's behalf to end the bombing war, and Bosnian Serb leaders Radovan Karadzic and Ratko Mladic were also removed from any diplomatic process in Bosnia by indictments. Former Tribunal president Antonio Cassese acknowledged this purposeful exclusion by indictment with pride.[41] By this route, also, all were effectively demonised before trial and conviction, and any NATO violence was justified in the media and public consciousness by Tribunal indictments.

On the other hand, in earlier years, when Milosevic was deemed useful to NATO as a negotiator in Bosnia, neither he nor Croatian leader Tudjman were indicted by the Tribunal for any crimes, although Milosevic was already well demonised, and in the ongoing Milosevic trial his alleged responsibility for crimes in those earlier years are a key focus of the prosecution case. U.N. diplomat Cedric Thornberry noted this politically based exemption of Milosevic and Tudjman, 'wooed diplomatically lest they pull the rug out from under the peace process,' and he objected that 'no political offer should be made that would suggest that any leader, credibly implicated in grave criminal activity, be immune from judicial prosecution.'[42] In effect, Thornberry was criticising the Tribunal back in 1996 for serving as a political arm of NATO.

Another huge political act carried out by Arbour, as well as her successor, Carla Del Ponte, was exempting NATO from any war crimes charges. The Security Council conveniently excluded from the war crimes subject to Tribunal jurisdiction what the Nuremberg tribunal had declared to be the 'supreme crime' – waging a war of aggression.[43] NATO could therefore attack Yugoslavia in violation of the U.N. Charter without thereby automatically committing a crime subject to Tribunal authority. Nevertheless, Article 5 of the Tribunal's Charter did make illegal 'crimes against humanity,' which includes 'murder' and 'other inhumane acts;' and Article 3 includes 'employment of poisonous weapons or other weapons calculated to cause unnecessary suffering,' and 'attack, or bombardment, by whatever means, of undefended towns, villages, dwellings, or buildings.' Articles 1 and 16 of the Tribunal's governing statute oblige it to prosecute any such illegal actions.[44]

How Arbour and Del Ponte wriggled out of even investigating NATO's war crimes, and the contrast with their rapid service for NATO, is amusing in the grossness of the difference between the two. Canadian law professor Michael Mandel describes how in May, 1999, he and a group of lawyers from North and South America filed a well-documented war crimes complaint against 68 NATO leaders, and travelled to The Hague to make the case to Arbour and then Del Ponte.[45] '[L]ike literally thousands around the world,' he said, 'we demanded that Arbour and Del Ponte enforce the law against NATO.' But Mandel says he eventually gave up when it became clear that, in his words, 'the tribunal was a hoax.'[46]

It took Del Ponte more than a year to announce, on June 2, 2000, that NATO was guilty of no crimes, 'and that (rather illogically) she was not opening an investigation into whether they had committed any.'[47] At that point she released a pre-investigation report of her Office of the Prosecutor (OTP), openly based on the belief that 'NATO and NATO countries' press statements are generally reliable and that explanations have been honestly given.' However, the OTP did acknowledge that NATO sometimes refused to answer questions – 'failed to address the specific incidents,' as they put it.[48] In which case, NATO not wanting an investigation, the OTP chose to not look any further, and simply dropped the subject. How is that for an independent judicial assessment?

In the indictment of Milosevic, Arbour used evidence about events that took place only six weeks earlier from a war zone, provided by an interested party (NATO), unverified by Tribunal personnel, and in conflict with her claim that she would never proceed on the basis of 'uncorroborated' evidence. But neither she nor Del Ponte could even 'open an investigation' into NATO's conduct during the war, after a year, with overwhelming evidence in the public domain pertaining to NATO actions that had killed many more than the numbers presented in the initial indictment of Milosevic (May 22, 1999). That indictment and the charge of 'crimes against humanity' were based on an alleged 385 killings for which Milosevic is said to have borne 'command responsibility;' but the *OTP Report* found that the 500 deaths attributable to NATO's actions were too few to rate – 'there is simply no evidence of the necessary crime base for charges of genocide or crimes against humanity.'[49] (It should also be noted that the first chief prosecutor of the ICTY, the sainted Richard Goldstone, vigorously defended the Tribunal's handling of the NATO charges in a debate with John Laughland, saying that the Tribunal simply 'held that there was not sufficient evidence against individuals to warrant further investigation,' when as we have indicated there was no serious initial investigation and the 500 deaths conceded by the OTP exceeded the total charged to Milosevic.)[50]

In examining possible NATO war crimes, time after time the OTP investigators would consider the evidence and then choose an interpretation favourable to NATO, as in the bombing of Serbian broadcasting facilities, or simply decide arbitrarily that since 'another interpretation is equally available' no investigation is needed (here in reference to NATO's April 12, 1999 bombing of a train crossing a bridge over the Grdelica Gorge, south of Belgrade).[51]. Michael Mandel gives a number of illustrations of this mode of exoneration, which, he says, 'comes as close as possible to being an actual NATO press release that might have been issued by Jamie Shea or James Rubin.'[52]

After Del Ponte took over from Arbour in mid-September 1999, she announced that the 'primary focus of the Office of the Prosecutor *must be* the investigation and prosecution of the five leaders of the Federal Republic of Yugoslavia who have already been indicted,' implicitly conceding that she didn't have enough evidence, but once again making clear her NATO-service priorities.[53] Despite the furious claims of 'genocide' in Kosovo by the NATO/Tribunal/media collective during the 78-day bombing war, the fewer than 5,000 bodies (from all causes and on all sides) found after the historically unprecedented postwar forensic search would hardly sustain a genocide charge against Milosevic.[54] Therefore, after his June 28, 2001 seizure and transport to The Hague, Del Ponte announced that charges against Milosevic would be expanded to his command responsibility for deaths in Croatia and Bosnia. The search was then on for evidence of deaths and, especially, proof of Milosevic's 'master plan.' This was a common Tribunal formula: Indict; flamboyantly publicize the charges; and then look for the evidence.

Further evidence of the Tribunal's service on behalf of NATO has been the fact that, from the very first, the Serbs were NATO's target, hence, the Tribunal's target as well. As early as the summer of 1992, German Foreign Minister Klaus Kinkel began accusing the Serbs of 'genocide;'[55] and in December 1992, just as the Tribunal was in process of formation, Acting U.S. Secretary of State Lawrence Eagleburger publicly named four Serb leaders – Milosevic, Karadzic, Mladic and Arkan – as targets of the imminent Tribunal, even invoking the need for a 'second Nuremberg.'[56] Tribunal President Gabrielle Kirk McDonald referred to Serbia as a 'rogue state,' and another Tribunal President Antonio Cassese expressed gratification that 'indictments' had made it impossible for Serb leaders to participate in negotiations. Cassese was not bothered by the Tribunal's abuse of indictments as a political instrument, and even Kosovo war supporter Geoffrey Robertson has observed that Cassese's 'presumption of their guilt, and agitation for their arrest, would have disqualified him for bias in many domestic legal systems.'[57]

The double standard in the Tribunal's dealing with the Serbs and others has been blatant. Serb paramilitary leader Arkan's indictment was made public in March 1999, but his Bosnian Muslim counterpart Naser Oric, who had bragged to the media about his killing of Serb civilians,[58] was not indicted until 2003, with only modest charges levied and its timing suggesting an attempt to create the appearance of balance.[59] The Republic of Serbian Krajina President Milan Martic was indicted as early as July 25, 1995 for – among other charges – a rocket-launched cluster-bomb attack on military targets in Zagreb in May 1995, on the ground that the rocket was 'not designed to hit military targets but to terrorise the civilians of Zagreb.' In Martic's case, the Tribunal went to some pains to investigate the nature, effects and anti-civilian character of cluster bombs, concluding that their use was inherently criminal – 'an anti-personnel weapon designed only to kill people.'[60] But NATO's cluster-bombing of Nis on May 7, 1999, which repeatedly hit a market and hospital far from any military target, killing at least 15 civilians in the process, produced no indictments.

Bosnian Serb General Stanislav Galic was found guilty by the Tribunal of 'inflicting terror on a civilian population,'[61] but the numerous admissions by NATO leaders that their bombing of Serbia in April and May 1999 was to inflict pain on – that is, to *terrorise* – that population and force surrender, carried out on a much larger scale than Galic's operations around Sarajevo, was of no interest to the Tribunal. And the massive ethnic cleansing of the Krajina by U.S.-advised Croatian forces in August, 1995, with many hundreds killed, led to no indictments until May 21, 2001 (though announced only in late July), when Del Ponte, aggressively pursuing the new Yugoslav government to extradite Milosevic and other Serb indictees, and apparently feeling a need to demonstrate her even-handedness, belatedly indicted a single Croatian military officer for his role in Operation Storm, General Ante Gotovina, along with General Rahim Ademi, an ethnic Albanian who served in the Croatian military and was involved in the slaughter of Serbs at Medak back in 1993.[62] (Before these indictments, no Croatian with command responsibility for Operation Storm had ever been indicted, and only Serbs had been indicted for their actions in Croatia's Krajina region.)

In the same mode of political bias, only Serb leaders have been charged with 'genocide' and the kind of top-down criminal responsibility for the acts of subordinates that we see in the Tribunal's charge that Milosevic masterminded a 'joint criminal enterprise' to ethnically cleanse non-Serbs from large areas of Croatia and Bosnia. Numerous mass killings by Bosnian Muslims – including imported Mujahedin whose specialty was beheading civilian victims[63] – and by the Croatian army and paramilitaries never caused the Tribunal to use the word 'genocide' or to attribute responsibility to, or indict, the late Croatian President Franjo Tudjman or his Bosnian Muslim counterpart Alija Izetbegovic.[64] And during her pretended look at NATO crimes, Del Ponte considered only the responsibility of NATO pilots and their immediate commanders, not the NATO decision-makers who decided to target the civilian infrastructure and population. The double standard here is dramatic.

How did Marlise Simons treat these manifestations of a Tribunal political agenda closely geared to U.S. and NATO public relations needs? Simons did not report on the Racak incident, but she did have an article on Arbour's March 31, 1999 announcement of the indictment of Arkan.[65] She transmitted Arbour's explanation for the belated release of the indictment – to warn those who might 'retain his services or obey his orders' and thus be 'tainted by their association with an indicted war criminal.' But Simons did not question this explanation, which is not compelling, and which treats an indicted but not-yet-convicted person as a 'criminal.' Nor did Simons mention that the release of the indictment was a public relations gift to NATO. Simons failed to call attention to the absence of any indictment of Naser Oric, Arkan's paramilitary counterpart serving the Bosnian Muslim side, and in fact she never mentioned Oric's name in any of the 120 articles that form the basis for this study.[66]

This convenient naiveté was even more dramatically evident in Simons' treatment of the May 22, 1999 indictment of Milosevic.[67] Here again, Simons gives Arbour's explanation of the rush to indict –

the fear that 'we might miss out' on getting him as a result of a peace deal – which she passes along without raising any question. Simons does not mention the Tribunal's failure to indict Milosevic in 1994-1995, when as Thornberry noted, Milosevic was seen by the leading NATO powers as a useful partner in a 'peace deal.' This allows her to suggest that 'only now do...American and European politicians...use the tribunal as a political weapon, threatening to hold perpetrators of atrocities accountable in The Hague,' which also makes it sound as if the Tribunal is an autonomous body being used by alien parties! The sheer injudicial character of rushing to indict, with a presumption of guilt even before the evidence is in, doesn't strike Simons.

Simons quotes Arbour acknowledging that NATO's aims here meshed with her own ('a coincidence of interests,' Arbour calls it), and this aura of independence is maintained and never challenged by Simons. She asserts that 'The indictment is now seen as a tribute to the tribunal's firmness,' without telling us who it is that has this vision and offers this tribute. Simons never hints that the timing of the indictment might be regarded as public relations service to NATO, although she mentions that U.S. and NATO officials welcomed Arbour's action. This was just a coincidence, as Arbour explained to her. As with Arbour's exploitation of the Racak incident to perform a public relations service on behalf of NATO, or Arbour's unsealing of the indictment of Arkan right after the start of the war, or Arbour's appearance with Robin Cook at a London press conference later in the war, or Arbour's rush to indict Milosevic as the war dragged on and began to go sour for NATO – Simons treats each as an isolated event, because connecting the dots between them, or performing any kind of serious analysis, would prove incompatible with peddling the official line.

Simons never deals with the Tribunal's exemption of NATO, and her colleagues at the *New York Times* treat that exemption with extreme brevity, featuring U.S. 'impatience' with this challenge, which never even reached the investigatory state. The *Times* reporters ignored the charges themselves and never referred to the comical Del Ponte and *OTP Report's* basis for rejecting even an investigation of NATO war crimes.[68] Only once does Simons approach the substance of the charges of NATO war crimes, when she says that NATO bombs 'hit the Chinese Embassy, a few bridges, a train full of civilian passengers, and a TV station.'[69] But no mention of the electrical and water facilities, marketplaces, nine hospitals, and over 300 schools damaged or destroyed. No mention of the innumerable factories producing civilian goods, museums, religious buildings, including early Christian and medieval churches. And no mention of the 500-3000 civilians killed during the bombing war. Simons' bias displayed in this aborted listing is dramatic, but her editors clearly didn't object.

Simons several times reported Tribunal developments that could be interpreted as showing that the Tribunal was not a political arm of NATO.[70] But she never once allowed this interpretation to be challenged or the neglected political model to be expounded, aside from a few phrases attributed to Slobodan Milosevic.

Alternative Model of the Tribunal as a 'Rogue Court'

The ICTY was established by the Security Council under Security Council Resolution 827 on May 25, 1993, under the claimed authority of Chapter VII of the U.N. Charter. But the Charter's Chapter VII gives the Security Council authority only on matters of *security*, and the argument that violations of humanitarian law 'constitute a threat to international peace and security' fails to provide a legally defensible basis for taking on a judicial function.[71] Ironically, Chapter VII requires all countries to cooperate with any ruling made under it, although it was only voted on by the Security Council. Meanwhile, the U.S. Congress, explaining why it was refusing to cooperate with the International Criminal Court, asserted that 'it is a fundamental principle of international law that a treaty is binding upon its parties only and that it does not create obligations for nonparties without their consent to be bound. The United States is not a party to the Rome statute and will not be bound by any of its terms.'[72] But no problem in binding countries to aiding the (illegally constituted) ICTY because it was under U.S. control and it was others who were coerced to cooperate without their assent. Marlise Simons and the *New York Times* have never addressed these issues.

It is an even more spectacular irony that the Tribunal was established in 1993, just after Eagleburger's public naming of Serb leaders to be brought to trial and during a period in which the United

States had begun 'the destruction of every single chance of peace, from the Vance-Owen in Bosnia to the farce of Rambouillet, to the bombing campaign itself.'[73] That is, the role of the Tribunal was to help the United States and its allies employ a purported 'bringing justice' as part of the propaganda apparatus to fend off peace, help dismantle Yugoslavia, and put Serbia in its place by war. Most of the deaths in Bosnia, Croatia and Kosovo occurred *after* the decisions were made to pursue 'justice' instead of peace. Recognition of the Tribunal's role in a policy relying ultimately on force was implicit in the statement of former Tribunal President Antonio Cassese, who noted that 'The political and diplomatic response [to the Balkans conflict] takes into account the exigencies and the tempo of the international community. The military response will come at the appropriate time.'[74] As Robert Hayden later observed, 'Instead of being victor's justice after the conflict, it [the Tribunal] is a tool meant to ensure victory during it.'[75] In fact, in the postwar phase, the Tribunal is serving to provide victors' justice – and a final apologetic for the war – as well.

Marlise Simons has never mentioned the Eagleburger statement of December, 1993, and, of course, she has never hinted at the possibility that the Tribunal's role was to facilitate war in the name of 'justice,' although she repeatedly transmits the prosecution and other prosecution-friendly statements about the importance of justice to the victims. She fails to mention that the alleged 'justice' objective is apparently not high on the priority lists of the populations in question, in contrast with U.S., NATO, Tribunal officials, as well as the media establishment.[76] And she consistently fails to address the matter of justice to victims outside the orbit of NATO interests, such as the ethnically-cleansed Serbs of the Krajina and Western Bosnian regions, the ethnically-cleansed Serbs and Roma from NATO-controlled Kosovo, and the refugees and beggared population of Serbia itself.

Most of the Tribunal prosecutors and judges have been drawn from the NATO countries, and all the important ones have been vetted by U.S. officials.[77] As the NATO powers are parties to the conflict, and even committed chargeable war crimes as well as engaging in the 'supreme crime' in the 78-day bombing war, there is a major conflict of interest built into the judicial structure of the Tribunal. As Hans

Koechler stated, 'If the "Tribunal" would have taken general legal standards of impartiality seriously, it would have been obliged to determine that there is a conflict of interest for "judges" from countries waging an undeclared war against Yugoslavia to sit on such a panel initiating "judicial" action against the Head of State of the country under attack.'[78] Marlise Simons has never considered this an issue or problem.

We have already mentioned the bias problems that follow from the Tribunal's source of funding, and the likelihood that Tribunal activity will be directed toward areas politically serviceable to the United States and other NATO powers. But another feature of funding bias is that the prosecution is likely to be given ample resources and political support while the defence is scanted. As Sellars points out, 'The defence is very much the poor relation at The Hague...the prosecution has been set up with a coordinating office and budget, the defence does not enjoy equivalent resources. It does not get much support from governments either.'[79]

As regards the judicial process more narrowly conceived, the Tribunal has violated Western judicial standards on a massive scale, as it has been free to create its own rules as it went along. Thus, its 1994 *Yearbook* states that 'The tribunal does not need to shackle itself with restrictive rules which have developed out of the ancient trial-by-jury system'[80]; and for Louise Arbour, 'The law, to me, should be creative and used to make things right.'[81] Yes, due process and other 'ancient' protections are inconvenient to aggressive prosecutors. John Laughland notes that 'the Tribunal dips into a pot-pourri of different legal systems from around the world. In one case, the tribunal defended itself against charges that it had illegally seized documents from the Bosnian government by saying that its procedures were compatible with the law in Paraguay.'[82]

Before examining some of the Tribunal's abuses, and Marlise Simons' (non)-treatment of them, in more detail, let us enumerate Laughland's non-exhaustive list of 'rogue court' procedures: (1) no right to bail or speedy trial; (2) defendants may be tried twice for the same crime [Article 25 of the Tribunal's statute]; (3) no right to a jury trial; (4) no independent appeal body; (5) admission of hearsay evidence; (6) confessions to be presumed free and voluntary unless the contrary is established by the prisoner [Article 92]; and (7) no definition of the burden of proof needed for a conviction, such as 'beyond reasonable doubt.'[83] Nowhere in her 120 articles does Marlise Simons mention, let alone challenge, these procedures – all of which are in violation of long-established principles of Western jurisprudence.

Another very important feature of Tribunal practice has been the use of the indictment as a political tool. In the 'ancient trial-by-jury' and due process systems of the West an indicted person is not by that fact a criminal but rather one for whom the evidence seems to justify a trial to determine guilt or innocence. For the Tribunal the indictment has been used to criminalise without trial, to remove the indictee from effective authority, and to discredit and demonise. As noted, Arbour used this weapon regularly as a political and propaganda tool, while piously claiming a belief that indictees are innocent till proven guilty. Even Geoffrey Robertson, a vocal supporter of NATO's 1999 war, has recognised that 'war required [Milosevic's] criminalisation, so The Hague prosecutor, Louise Arbour, was summoned to London to be handed by UK Foreign Secretary Robin Cook some NSA/GCHQ intercepts she had long requested.'[84] Milosevic was indicted shortly thereafter. Back in 1995, Arbour's predecessor, Richard Goldstone, admitted to purposefully indicting Karadzic and Mladic to exclude them from the imminent Dayton talks,[85] but not Milosevic, now under indictment as the alleged 'architect' of the events for which Karadzic and Mladic were indicted. Marlise Simons has never acknowledged the ICTY's politicisation of indictments, nor has she expressed the slightest concern over their use for advance criminalisation.

The Tribunal's prosecutors have been very media oriented, with the criminalising indictments central to their effort to mobilise the media in support of the Tribunal. Among other incidents, in June, 2001, Del Ponte announced that Milosevic would soon be indicted for additional crimes[86], an action that had no function except to keep Tribunal business in the public eye and create a public and moral environment biased against the defendant. Cassese openly employed the same tactic of going to the public about the 'indicted criminals' in order to force political action.[87] Similarly, Richard Goldstone frankly acknowledged that journalists 'responded to my calls for positive and supportive coverage' of the Tribunal.[88] Again, the violations of judicial principles in this call and mobilisation were notorious, but entirely consistent with Tribunal procedures. Marlise Simons almost certainly didn't need Goldstone's call to follow the Tribunal party line, and she has never noticed any anomalies or departures from honourable judicial practice in publicity mongering or courtroom procedures. In fact, as far as she is aware, everyone working for the Tribunal bends over backwards to avoid publicity and the appearance of a conflict of interest![89]

The first case tried by the Tribunal, involving the Bosnian Serb Dusko Tadic, affords us an excellent illustration of both the Tribunal's unjudicial practices and Marlise Simons' extreme bias. Only one witness ever testified to having actually seen Tadic commit an atrocity, an anonymous Bosnian Serb sent to the Tribunal after his seizure by the Bosnian Muslims. The defence was able to show that the witness lied, at which point he confessed that he had been forced to lie, and was trained on his testimony, by his Bosnian Muslim captors. The prosecutor withdrew the witness's testimony, but the Trial Chamber never asked why the prosecutor had failed to discover the basic facts about the witness; Robert Hayden, who was an expert witness in this case, claims that 'some parts of the witness's story seem to indicate the Prosecutor's office might also have been involved in training him to give false testimony.'[90] The Tribunal then denied the witness's appeal for refuge and sent him back to the Bosnian Muslim government, where he was given a ten-year sentence for 'genocide' based on a confession he says was extracted by torture.

The Tadic case involved charges under Article 2 of the ICTY statute, which applies only to persons 'caught up in an international armed conflict.' In a preliminary hearing, the ICTY Appeals Chamber found the Bosnian conflict to be both internal *and* external, and argued that if it was found to be solely 'international' (i.e., external), an 'absurd' conclusion would follow: That only Bosnian Muslims, not Bosnian Serbs, could be 'protected persons' under the statute. The Trial Chamber, following the reasoning in the International Court of Justice in its 1986 decision *Nicaragua v. United States of America.*, found that the Bosnian Serbs were not *de facto* organs or agents of Belgrade. The prosecutor appealed the decision, and won, with the Appeals Chamber now accepting precisely the conclusion that it had earlier found 'absurd,' and arguing that mere 'participation' in planning and supervising military operations constitutes 'overall control.' It justified this position on the grounds of the need to protect civilians and 'realism...which disregards legal formalities.' Apart from the brazenness of this self-contradiction and rewriting of legal rules, 'The ICTY Appeals Chamber has thus clearly indicated that fairness of the proceedings for defendants is not high in its concerns,' Robert Hayden concludes.[91]

Hayden also points out that this ICTY ruling and disregard of 'legal formalities' would not only make the United States responsible for all the crimes of the Nicaraguan contras, it would also make it responsible for its 'de facto agents' in the Croatian army's Operation Storm, the assault on the Krajina Serbs in August, 1995, carried out with the approval and participation of U.S. officials and closely affiliated 'private' firms.[92] Naturally, the Tribunal, which couldn't even open an investigation into NATO's direct war crimes, would never make this connection involving mere *de facto* agents killing the wrong victims.

In her reports on the Tadic trial, Simons devoted a great deal of space to summarising the prosecution's charges and description of the Omarska prison camp as a 'concentration camp.'[93] But reading Simons, one would never be aware of the fact that Tadic was sentenced to 20 years, although acquitted of personal responsibility for any murders. There is no mention of the fact that the one witness who claimed to actually *see* Tadic kill was eventually withdrawn by the prosecution after having been found to be fabricating evidence, and after confessing to having been coerced and trained on what to say. Reporting this would throw unfavourable light on Tribunal processes, and Simons regularly ignores such negatives.

On the issue of whether Tadic would be subject to Article 2 charges based on the finding of the conflict in Bosnia as internal or external, Simons does not evaluate the arguments on the difference between 'control' and 'participation,' nor does she discuss the facts about the relation between the Yugoslav and Bosnian armed forces. The struggles between Milosevic and the Bosnian Serbs and their conflicting interests in the peace efforts in the years 1992-1995 – as described, for example, in Lord David Owen's *Balkan Odyssey*[94] – are of no interest to Simons. She doesn't mention the arguments given by the Tribunal judges who at first disputed the control claim, and there is no evidence that she ever bothered to hear or read them or the testimony of Robert Hayden.[95] She just takes it for granted that the NATO-friendly position is correct: She says that 'most Western governments' would claim that the Bosnian Serb warfare was 'orchestrated from Belgrade.'[96] So any contrary findings brought before the Tribunal are *ipso facto* wrong and perverse.

And in a remarkable and stupid *ad hominem* attack, Simons smears the dissident judges as tools of Milosevic, claiming that their finding of only participation rather than control was a Milosevic 'stratagem' and 'victory': 'Mr. Milosevic has now by some accounts hoodwinked two of the tribunal's judges.' For these 'some accounts' she seems to be relying on 'diplomats' and an unnamed 'international lawyer.' The heroine in her morality tale here is Judge Gabrielle Kirk McDonald, the Clinton State Department's contribution to international justice, and former (and post-Tribunal) director and counsel of Freeport-McMoRan Copper & Gold Inc., who stood firmly by the NATO position in this voting. Simons also quotes Gow, who is NATO-friendly, but completely ignores Hayden's extensive arguments supporting the position of the 'hoodwinked' judges.

We might also note that the argument accepted by McDonald and Simons, that the participation of the Yugoslav government with the Bosnian Serbs in the form of funding support and occasional joint operations was proof of Yugoslav control, would point to U.S. and NATO-power control of the Tribunal itself. Not surprisingly Marlise Simons has never made this analogy or drawn this inference.

Over the course of the prosecution's seemingly endless parade of witnesses, which totalled 296 in all before it rested its case on February 25, 2004, almost 25 months after the case opened, the prosecution frequently cultivated a sense of anticipation that this witness, or that, would be the one to serve up the *coup de grâce* for Milosevic. One such witness was the three-time President of an independent Slovenia, Milan Kucan – the man who 'led the Slovene delegation out of a Communist Party congress in 1990,' Simons notes, and declared independence from Yugoslavia the summer of the following year.[97] Simons' relatively brief coverage of Kucan's single day before the Tribunal[98] touched on a key moment of Milosevic's cross-examination, when Milosevic asked Kucan, 'Why did you need this war? You opted for violence....' But such a question Simons balanced with Kucan's testimony that Slovenia was acting in response to Milosevic's threats that 'borders might be redrawn by force,' along with her own gloss on Kucan's testimony that 'it had become clear to him that Mr. Milosevic would use every means, even violence, to keep all Serbs in a Yugoslav state.' Simons failed to report the one question to which Milosevic returned, over and over again: 'Why did you attack the JNA in Slovenia?'[99] That is, why did the Kucan Government's forces attack the forces of the Federal Government, given the latter's constitutional responsibility to defend the territorial integrity of Yugoslavia, and ensure domestic order?[100] Simons also failed to report the extensive documentation that Milosevic tried to present on the violence that the Slovene Territorial Defence Units and paramilitaries had perpetrated against the regulars of the JNA and family members after the declaration of Slovenian independence,[101] or Milosevic's claim that the Yugoslav Constitutional Court had ruled no less than 27 times that the route adopted by Slovenia's political leadership towards independence was incompatible with the Federal Constitution.[102] Nor did Simons mention Milosevic's contention that before and after Slovenia's so-called Ten Day War, the Kucan Government was involved in the shipment of arms to the far more hotly contested breakaway republics of Croatia and Bosnia-Herzegovina, and the Serbian province of Kosovo.[103] Indeed, as far as Simons was concerned, each of the antagonists accused the 'other of warmongering as they relived their fight of more than a decade ago' – and that was it. In keeping with her standard practice, however, Simons did remind *Times* readers that Milosevic 'is widely held to be most responsible for leading the Serbs into conflicts in Croatia and Bosnia that took more than 200,000 lives.'[104]

Zoran Lilic and Borisav Jovic, two ethnic Serbs and former close colleagues of Milosevic whose appearances as prosecution witnesses received the same kind of promotion as Kucan's, also gave testimonies that proved equally deflating. Indeed, Lilic's three days before the

A Study in Propaganda

Tribunal happened to coincide with what appears to have been a manoeuvre by the increasingly desperate Office of the Prosecution to divert attention away from Lilic's actual testimony, in which the former Yugoslav President (1993-1997) rejected the core of the prosecution's contention that Milosevic's guilt for 'genocide' in Bosnia-Herzegovina rests with his 'command responsibility' for the alleged massacre of some 7,000 Bosnian Muslims following the evacuation of the Srebrenica 'safe area' in July 1995. 'I am sure he could not have issued an order of that kind,' Lilic said during his extensive first day's testimony. 'I am quite certain [Milosevic] didn't have influence on a decision of that kind.'[105] But Simons reduced the whole of Lilic's three days of testimony to a total of 16 quoted words spread over two short paragraphs at the very end of her article. Instead, Simons swallowed the Office of the Prosecutor's bait, its revelation of a document that 'may prove to be crucial evidence in support of their case that the former Yugoslav president is guilty of genocide.' First published on the webpage of the highly-compromised Institute for War & Peace Reporting, the alleged document 'not only puts Serbian special police at the massacre site but also provides a direct link to Mr. Milosevic,' Simons reported. '[T]his is the first such document relating to the July 1995 massacre,' an anonymous 'official in the prosecutor's office' told her.[106] In this manner Simons and the *New York Times* helped the prosecution salvage the Lilic bust by rushing to print news about an alleged secret document proving Serb perfidy, a document whose shelf life proved to be exceedingly short, once its real purpose had been served.

As for Borisav Jovic, the former Serbian representative on the collective Federal Presidency for Yugoslavia during the period the Federation dissolved into wars, neither Simons nor any of her colleagues with the *New York Times* reported his three days of testimony before the Tribunal in November 2003, which also hurt the prosecution case by denying Milosevic command responsibility for Bosnian killings but which also scoffed at the crucial prosecution claim of a plan for a 'Greater Serbia.'[107] Jovic also discussed the matter of 'ethnic cleansing,' agreeing that the practice existed, but denying that Milosevic's policies ever supported it.[108] Jovic gave his testimony despite the fact that in its indictments of Milosevic, Jovic's name appears right alongside those 'individuals participating in [the] joint criminal enterprise.'[109] This should make Jovic 'clearly wary of incriminating himself,' in the view of one observer,[110] with the Tribunal holding the threat of his potential indictment over his head, actionable at any time.[111] But as with Lilic's earlier testimony, this was not news fit to print on the pages of the *New York Times*.

In one of the most remarkable moments in the trial of Milosevic, the prosecution brought on as a witness Radomir Markovic, the former head of State Security of Yugoslavia, who came to the Hague after having been held for 17 months in a Serb jail. On cross-examination, he completely repudiated the testimony he had made to his jailers, contending that Milosevic had not only had nothing to do with any crimes committed in Kosovo but had tried to curb them and punish any violators. Most interesting, he testified that he had been threatened with criminal prosecution unless he agreed to testify against Milosevic, and was offered bribes for cooperation. Marlise Simons mentions that Markovic was a prosecution witness in her first article on his testimony,[112] but when in cross-examination he exonerated Milosevic from criminal activity and described the bribe-threat combination that he had faced, Simons's follow-up article is very short and evasive.[113] She no longer mentions that he was a prosecution witness, and she completely suppresses his bribe-threat claims. He is now portrayed as a friend of Milosevic who 'has sided with his boss.' In both articles dealing with Markovic's testimony, Simons gets in sentences on 'shocking details about atrocities against ethnic Albanians' that have no connection with the main topics of the articles.

In many cases the bribe-threat combination that Markovic describes and Simons cannot acknowledge in his case has been effective. The threat was increasingly effective as targets became aware of the fact that the deck was stacked against them – that Tribunal rules were flexible, that traditional rules against hearsay, double-jeopardy and rights of appeal were inoperative, that NATO-agent judges and prosecutors were free to pursue and punish Serbs without constraint as 'the fix was on.'[114] Under these conditions, and with the post-Milosevic Serbian government now both cooperative and under intense pressure to cooperate without limit, resistance to the blandishments of 'confessions' and 'plea-bargaining' weakened. A major problem, however, has been whether the confessions might be false and the newly-minted claims of the (almost invariably) Serb villain were true or whether he was saying what he felt would diminish his sentence. In the Bulgarian Connection case, Agca confessed to Bulgarian and KGB guilt, after many months of interrogations and disclosure of the desired line of confession. It is now clear that he was lying, but the *New York Times* and its colleagues lapped up the lies with uncritical zeal.

And now, with a new problematic on confessions, it is notable how similarly uncritical Simons and her *Times* colleagues are on plea-bargaining. Not once in 120 articles does she suggest the possibility of coaching and systematic false witness based on the plea-bargaining process. She treats it as a purely innocent and excellent innovation designed to speed things up a bit, and she asserts that the new cooperation on the part of the indictees is based above all on their new sense that the Tribunal is fair!'[115] Any other possible explanation is unmentioned.

The issue was posed once again in the case of Bosnian Serb intelligence officer Momir Nikolic, who confessed to Serb crimes at Srebrenica in exactly the form desired by the prosecution: 'with cool precision,' as Simons described, quoting directives that 'the life of the enemy must be made unbearable,' and describing the actions taken in preparation for mass executions, although it turns out that Nikolic himself didn't witness any executions.[116] He and a colleague helped organise digging mass graves, and later digging up bodies and reburying them in secret sites – though no explanation is offered as to why they didn't bury them in secret sites in the first place, or how a site is made 'secret.'

A problem arose in Nikolic's testimony, however, when on cross-examination it was demonstrated, and he himself acknowledged, that he had lied in claiming his presence at a particular massacre. Simons mentions this incongruous fact, very briefly, placing it near the end of a long article that paraphrased Nikolic as saying that 'he accepted more guilt, fearing that the plea agreement might fall through.'[117] This might suggest the possibility that Nikolic's other claims could have been equally untrue and dictated by the demands of those offering him his plea bargain. But this, along with the possibility of witness coaching, are not discussed by Simons, as she hastened on to more important matters.

Prosecution witness protection was one of the specialities of Milosevic trial judge Richard May. From the beginning, instead of leaning over backward to help the unrepresented accused, May not only displayed open hostility toward him, he limited and interfered with his cross-examination, while giving great freedom and protection to the prosecution and its witnesses. The experienced Canadian trial lawyer Edward Greenspan was outraged at the fact that May violated 'the well-known principle that no judge can arbitrarily set a time limit on, or interfere with, a cross examination.' Within an hour-and-a-half of the beginning of Milosevic's first cross-examination, 'May impatiently asks: 'How much longer do you think you're going to be with this witness'?...The first witness of what is to be a lengthy trial, and the judge is putting time limits on the accused. May doesn't even feign impartiality, or, indeed, interest.' Greenspan is also shocked at May's admonition to Milosevic not to cross-examine 'as a way of harassing or intimidating witnesses.' Brutality is 'calculated to unnerve, confuse, but ultimately to expose. Cross-examination is a duel between counsel and the witness. The only weapon the defendant has is the right to ask questions.'[118]

One observer of Judge May's methods in the first week of June 2002, the British paralegal Ian Johnson, noted that 'at no time during this process did the judge...stipulate a time limit on the prosecution. Yet when it was the turn of Mr. Milosevic to cross-examine the witness, Judge May would instruct that a time limit be put on the proceedings.' Johnson reports that when the prosecution witness Mr. Buyo, a KLA commander in the Racak area, was put under pressure by Milosevic, who caught him in a contradiction and with the witness clearly in trouble, Judge May instructed: 'Move on Mr Milosevic, you have laboured this point enough.' As Johnson points out, 'Mr Buyo was off the hook.' In the cross-examination of another claimed eyewitness to a massacre of civilians, who said that the Serb forces had separated the women and children from the men and then proceeded to execute all of them, Milosevic asked him why they bothered to do the separation if they were going to kill them all. But Judge May

A Study in Propaganda

interjected: 'I don't think you can expect the witness to know that,' when of course Milosevic was probing possible false testimony. This probe was terminated by the judge.

With another witness, who claimed to have overheard threatening conversations by Serb commanders from his position hidden in an attic, Milosevic got him into difficulties based on noise and distance, in the midst of which Judge May says: 'Move on Mr. Milosevic, the witness has told you his position,' protecting the witness from serious embarrassment and from being discredited.

In another case, where the witness claimed her town had been hit by Yugoslav airplanes, and displayed a knowledge of technical names of weaponry that was implausible and suggested coaching, when Milosevic tried to press this point, May simply cut him off: 'She has answered your question [about who told her to say what she did]. She said nobody did and that is what she saw, and that's her evidence. No point arguing about it.'[119]

Even more dramatic was Judge May's handling of the testimony of William Walker on June 11-12, 2002. Although Walker ranged far and wide, even covering his estimate of Milosevic's 'general attitude,' May never interrupted him once in nearly two hours of testimony. Although the 'Racak massacre' claim was the basis of 45 charges of murder against Milosevic in the indictment for Kosovo, and although Walker's credibility as the main driver of that claim was important and relevant, May announced in advance a limit of three hours to cross-examination, and then proceeded to interrupt Milosevic's questioning *over 70 times*. His deference to 'Ambassador' Walker, as May called him, was striking, as May actively prevented a serious cross-examination that might have challenged Walker's credibility and exposed his lies. If Walker simply dodged a question with 'I don't recall,' May protected him from any further questions. May refused to allow Milosevic to contrast Walker's immediate conclusion that the finding of the bodies at Racak constituted a massacre with Walker's foot-dragging in the case of murders in El Salvador, when he served as the U.S. Ambassador to the country in 1989: 'Your attempt to discredit this witness with events so long ago the Trial Chamber has ruled as irrelevant,' May insisted.[120] In short, this episode of witness protection and judicial abuse would by itself provide very strong grounds for throwing out the trial as unfair in a court system of integrity.

May frequently allowed prosecution witnesses to testify at length about personal experiences, and to attack Milosevic, usually without supportive and verifiable evidence, and to recite hearsay experiences. In Mahmut Bakali's testimony on February 18, 2002, the witness cited what a local Serb official claimed to have heard Milosevic might have said about Kosovo – twice-removed hearsay – without judicial interference.[121] By contrast, Judge May would not allow Milosevic to cite articles from *Le Monde* and *Le Figaro* that raised serious doubts about the nature of the Racak incident in his cross-examination of William Walker – our meticulous judge insisted that the reporters themselves would have to be brought to testify, rather than the articles they had written. Because of the absence of any ban on hearsay, and judicial bias, it has been estimated that 'over ninety percent' of the evidence cited in the Tribunal proceedings is from hearsay sources.[122] The Tribunal has also decided that in cases of rape or sex crimes, 'no corroboration of the victim's testimony shall be required.'[123]

We should also mention that Judge May repeatedly told witnesses that they should not communicate with others during the period when they were testifying, as in the hearing on November 13, 2003: 'Lieutenant Colonel, could I remind you, please, as we remind all witnesses, not to speak to anybody about your evidence until it's over.' But with General Wesley Clark, he allowed the U.S. government to force a closed session and to redact the testimony before release, and Clark was permitted to speak to others during the course of his testimony. Clark could even phone Bill Clinton in the midst of his testimony, get him to send a fax letter, and read that letter in court. As noted, May would not allow Milosevic to introduce articles from *Le Monde* and *Le Figaro*, requiring from him the physical presence of the reporters. In response to one simple question by Milosevic on a statement about Clark by his superior General Henry Shelton, Clark launched into a ten minute monologue of self adulation, without any interruption by Judge May. May would also not allow Milosevic to ask questions about NATO's intervention, whether the attack on Yugoslavia was legal, or whether it was a war. He could not ask questions challenging Clark's credibility, or anything not directly responsive to Clark verbal claims. Again, as with the William Walker testimony, this would be the basis for declaration of an unfair trial in an honest judicial system. But Marlise Simons and her *Times* colleague Elaine Sciolino never noticed,[124] and never sought comment from anybody who would challenge this almost humorous travesty of the judicial process.[125]

Marlise Simons' treatment of Judge May and his courtroom practice was entirely favourable and without a single note of criticism. Sober, polite, patient, giving Milosevic more time than the prosecution. Simons found that 'a consensus is growing that Mr. Milosevic is being treated fairly in the courtroom,' although once again she provides no source or evidence for the alleged consensus.[126] The idea that, as Edward Greenspan indicated, it was outrageous to arbitrarily limit cross-examination time, never struck Simons, nor did she ever mention the failure of May to interrupt Walker once while doing it incessantly with Milosevic. She never once found his protection of witnesses or acceptance of hearsay from them, but much harsher treatment of Milosevic, problematic. Milosevic, on the other hand, is repeatedly criticised by Simons for 'filibustering,' 'stalling,' 'playing to an audience,' 'often trying to bend the rules' and even for 'demanding as much time to question a witness as the prosecution' – a display of profound ignorance about the judicial process.[127] Given the facts, even in the summary form presented here, this apologetic for May, along with steady carping at Milosevic's courtroom performance, reflects deep bias.

Concluding Note

In February, 2004, it was reported that the United States and other NATO powers were now pressing the Tribunal to remove the authority to initiate prosecutions from prosecutor Carla Del Ponte, and transfer this authority to the Tribunal judges; and that in the interim, the judges were not giving approval to Del Ponte's requests to commence further prosecutions. It was alleged that Del Ponte had been too aggressive in seeking indictees, whereas the United States was eager to scale down Tribunal operations and would be satisfied to just dispose of Milosevic, along with the Bosnian Serb wartime leader Radovan Karadzic and General Ratko Mladic, and close the Tribunal down.[128] Does this mini-struggle and need to constrain Del Ponte demonstrate Tribunal autonomy? No, it does not. Puppets frequently get an inflated view of their importance, and have to be slapped down by their principals.[129] Moreover, it is clear in this case that the principals are well on their way to revamping the decision-making structure of the Tribunal to meet their latest priorities.

Anybody reading *Not Guilty: Report of the Commission of Inquiry Into the Charges Made Against Leon Trotsky in the Moscow Trials* (1937), written by a group chaired by John Dewey,[130] can only be struck by the frequent parallels between Soviet and ICTY principles and court procedure. The Dewey Commission stressed the political and public relations function of the Moscow trials,[131] and the 'prearranged scheme' and plan to prove that a single bad man (Trotsky) was guilty.[132] The Commission argued that there was no real effort to establish truth, but merely to prove guilt.[133] It stressed the self-interest of the accusers.[134]

We have tried to show that the International Criminal Tribunal for the Former Yugoslavia has been a thorough-going servant of NATO, and that the political model of the ICTY fits its history and record very closely. We have also tried to show that its judicial practice has continuously violated traditional Western standards almost across the board, even apart from its selective and politicised (and hyperpublicised) indictments and trials.

The *New York Times*'s Marlise Simons, however, has portrayed the Tribunal as a marvel of Western justice, by denying or (mainly) evading the evidence of its political role and judicial malpractice. We find it hard to believe that the Soviet media at the time of the Moscow show trials in 1936 could have done a better job on behalf of the Soviet prosecutor than Simons has done for the ICTY's prosecutors. In fact, Simons has almost surely done the better job, because she does quote Milosevic, even if briefly and with derisive comments; and while hugely biased, she is not frenzied and hysterical in her abuse of the villains. There is even a very small trickle of inconvenient facts within the overwhelming barrage of Tribunal-supportive propaganda. But this is effective propaganda – not propaganda that ordinary people will easily see through. As evidence gradually breaks through the 'coercive consensus' that now prevails, and upsets claims

A Study in Propaganda

of the Tribunal that have been conduited by Simons (though she is far from alone), we believe that, as with the Bulgarian Connection, Simons and the *New York Times* will not rush to straighten out their brain-washed readers.

Footnotes
1. For details, see Edward S. Herman and Noam Chomsky, *Manufacturing Consent: The Political Economy of the Mass Media* (New York: Pantheon, 1988 and 2002), Ch. 4 and Introduction to 2002 revised edition, pp. 143-167; and pp. xxvii-xxix.
2. Stacy Sullivan, 'Milosevic's Willing Executioners,' *New Republic*, May 10, 1999. Remaining faithful to this vision of the Serbs' ultimate responsibility for the wars, the next issue of the *New Republic* followed with Harvard academic Daniel Jonah Goldhagen's defense of NATO's war against, and eventual occupation of, Serbia, on the grounds that 'by supporting or condoning Milosevic's eliminationist politics, [the majority of the Serbian people] have rendered themselves both legally and morally incompetent to conduct their own affairs....' 'A New Serbia,' May 17, 1999.
3. For two examples of the 'party line' or standard media version: First, the journalist Christopher Hitchens asserts that these were wars 'between all those who favor ethnic and religious partition and all those who oppose it.' ('Ethnic cleansing in Bosnia,' *The Nation*, October 23, 1995.) This is a comic strip version of recent Balkan history. A second comes from the Tribunal's indictment of Milosevic for the wars that consumed the former Republic of Bosnia-Herzegovina, in which the Tribunal charges him with having begun to participate in a 'joint criminal enterprise' no later than August 1, 1991 (i.e., at least seven months before the Muslim-led government in Sarajevo declared the Republic's independence from Yugoslavia), the explicit purpose of which was the 'forcible and permanent removal of the majority of non-Serbs, principally Bosnian Muslims and Bosnian Croats, from large areas of the Republic of Bosnia and Herzegovina.' (*The Prosecutor of the Tribunal Against Slobodan Milosevic, Indictment [for Bosnia-Herzegovina]*, Case No. IT-01-51-I, November 22, 2001, pars. 5-9, <http://www.un.org/icty/indictment/english/mil-ii011122e.htm>.)
4. Among the most helpful contesting sources on the breakup of Yugoslavia are: Tariq Ali, ed., *Masters of the Universe: NATO's Balkan Crusade* (New York: Verso, 2000); Steven L. Burg and Paul S. Shoup, *The War in Bosnia-Herzegovina: Ethnic Conflict and International Intervention* (Armonk, New York: M. E. Sharp, 1999); David Chandler, *Bosnia: Faking Democracy After Dayton* (Sterling, Virginia: Pluto Press, 1999); Noam Chomsky, *The New Military Humanism: Lessons from Kosovo* (Monroe, Maine: Common Courage Press, 1999); Lenard J. Cohen, *Broken Bonds: Yugoslavia's Disintegration and Balkan Politics in Transition*, 2nd. Ed. (Boulder, Colorado: Westview Press, 1995);

Lenard J. Cohen, *Serpent in the Bosom: The Rise and Fall of Slobodan Milosevic* (Boulder, Colorado: Westview Press, 2001); Philip Hammond and Edward S. Herman, eds., *Degraded Capability: The Media and the Kosovo Crisis* (Sterling, Virginia: Pluto Press, 2000); Robert M. Hayden, *Blueprints for a House Divided: The Constitutional Logic of the Yugoslav Conflicts* (Ann Arbor, Michigan: University of Michigan Press, 1999); Robert M. Hayden, 'Biased "Justice": Humanrightsism and the International Criminal Tribunal for the Former Yugoslavia,' *Cleveland State Law Review*, 1999; Edward S. Herman and David Peterson, 'Morality's Avenging Angels,' in David Chandler, ed., *Rethnking Human Rights: Critical Approaches to International Politics* (London: Palgrave Macmillan, 2002), pp. 196-216; Diana Johnstone, *Fools' Crusade: Yugoslavia, NATO and Western Delusions* (New York: Monthly Review Press, 2002); Michael Mandel, 'Politics and Human Rights In International Criminal Law: Our Case Against NATO And The Lessons To Be Learned From It,' *Fordham International Law Journal*, 25: 95-128 (November, 2001); Michael Mandel, *How America Gets Away With Murder: Illegal Wars, Collateral Damage and Crimes Against Humanity* (London: Pluto, June 2004); Kirsten Sellars, *The Rise and Rise of Human Rights* (London: Sutton Publishing, 2002); and Susan L. Woodward, *Balkan Tragedy: Chaos and Dissolution After the Cold War* (Washington, D.C.: The Brookings Institution, 1995).

5. Raymond Bonner, *Weakness and Deceit: U.S. Policy and El Salvador* (New York: Times Books, 1984), Ch. 16; Edward Herman and Peter Rothberg, 'Media Thugs Slug It Out,' *Lies of Our Times*, June 1993, pp. 3-4. As for the dramatic drop off in the appearance of David Binder's byline in reports about the former Yugoslavia in the *New York Times*, a search of the Nexis database shows that for the years 1990-1993, the *Times* ran Binder's reports on Yugoslavia a total of 146 times, 51 of these having appeared during 1993 alone; and yet after 1993, Binder's reporting on Yugoslavia fell to only three times in 1994, and never more than twice during any subsequent year.

6. Several of Simons' articles were co-authored with other *Times* reporters, and we will refer occasionally to articles by these other reporters to show that on the points with which they deal, they also adhere to the party line, virtually without exception.

7. On the role of human rights organizations – most notably the U.S.-based Human Rights Watch – and their moral advocacy on behalf of NATO's military intervention in Yugoslavia and the proceedings of the Tribunal, see Sellars, op. cit., Ch. 9.

8. The 120 articles that comprise our Simons universe were extracted from the Nexis database by performing a 'Power' search of the *New York Times* through December 31, 2003. In the terminology of the Nexis database, we used the following search parameters:

* Byline(Marlise w/3 Simons) and Tribunal or The Hague and Yugoslavia or Serbia or Slovenia or Croatia or Bosnia or Kosovo and date bef 2004

9. Marlise Simons, 'War Crimes Trial Seeks to Define the Balkan Conflicts,'

A Study in Propaganda

New York Times, May 12, 1996. – We discuss below Simons' hugely biased treatment of the issue.

10. Cohen, *Serpent in the Bosom*, p. 380. Among other establishment truths that Simons repeats uncritically and frequently is the claim that Milosevic was driven by his desire for a 'Greater Serbia,' even a living space entirely freed of non-Serbs. That he was being pressed by Serb minorities who found themselves stranded within the newly independent states of Croatia and Bosnia-Herzegovina to help them stay within a 'Shrinking Yugoslavia' never occurs to Simons. See Johnstone, op. cit., pp. 32ff.

11. For illustrations of these confident assertions that 'we have the evidence,' which they most assuredly did *not* have, see Herman and Chomsky, op. cit., pp. 154-157.

12. For example, 'Prosecutors said their cases against the most senior Serb leaders...were solid' (Simons, May 18, 1997); 'the changes have engendered a rare sense of excitement in the sober high-security building' (Simons, April 10, 2000); and 'Milosevic, insiders say, has taken great pains to avoid written orders' (Simons, June 20, 2003).

13. Cedric Thornberry, a U.N. official with long experience in Bosnia, wrote in 1996 that the consensus evolving 'in parts of the international liberal media' that the Serbs were 'the only villains...did not correspond to the perceptions of successive senior U.N personnel in touch with daily events throughout the area.' 'Saving the war crimes tribunal,' *Foreign Policy*, Fall, 1996, p. 78. Among many other documents making the same point on the basis of very strong evidence, see Raymond K. Kent, 'Contextualizing Hate: The Hague Tribunal, the Clinton Administration and the Serbs,' 1996, <http://emperors-clothes.com/misc/kent.htm>.

14. For example, Simons writes that Milosevic 'faces a succession of witnesses, many of them humble villagers, who have traveled from Kosovo to The Hague to confront him and accuse him of destroying their lives.' 'Revising Memories Of Yet Another Evil,' *New York Times*, September 22, 2002.

15. Just considering here Bosnia and Croatia, on May 24, 1993, the Yugoslav government submitted a Letter to the U.N. on 'War Crimes and Crimes and Genocide in Eastern Bosnia...Committed Against the Serb Population from April 1992 to April 1993.' This document describes the 'almost complete ethnic cleansing of Serbs' from Srebrenica before the autumn of 1992, and lists 12 settlements and 39 villages destroyed and burnt down by Bosnian Muslim forces, with about 1,200 killed and between 2,800 and 3,200 injured. The almost complete ethnic cleansing of Serbs from Srebrenica described in this document is supported by the monthly reports of the U.N. High Commissioner for Refugees, which also show that all the so-called 'safe areas' (i.e., rendered safe for Bosnian Muslims) had been substantially cleansed of Serbs before July 1995. Half of the Serb population of the overall area around Srebrenica had been driven out by this time. This report includes scores of affidavits from Serb victims, who were often able to name the Bosnian

Muslims who attacked them.

An even more extensive document produced by the Serbian Council Information Center was titled, 'Persecution of Serbs and Ethnic Cleansing in Croatia 1991-1998.' This document provided massive data on killings, destruction of homes, and enforced flight, similar in character to the data put forward by the Tribunal in its focus on the persecution of Bosnian Muslims. These documents have never been mentioned in the *New York Times*, and the perpetrators of these crimes have never been indicted by the Tribunal.

16. Ian Fisher and Marlise Simons, 'Defiant, Milosevic Begins His Defense By Assailing NATO,' *New York Times*, February 15, 2002.

17. See Philip Hammond, 'Moral Combat: Advocacy Journalists and the New Humanitarianism,' in Chandler, ed., *Rethinking Human Rights*, pp. 176-195.

18. Edward L. Greenspan, 'This is a lynching,' *National Post*, March 13, 2002.

19. Fisher and Simons, op. cit.

20. See U.N. Security Council Resolution 827, May 25, 1993, <http://www1.umn.edu/humanrts/peace/docs/scres827.html>.

21. David J. Scheffer, Congressional Testimony on the Establishment of a Permanent International Criminal Court before the Committee on Foreign Relations of the U.S. Senate, Federal Document Clearing House, July 23, 1998. Scheffer was then serving as the liberal Democratic Clinton Administration's Ambassador-at-Large for War Crimes Issues.

22. Jamie Shea, 'Daily NATO Briefing,' NATO Headquarters, Brussels, Belgium, Federal News Service, May 17, 1999.

23. Sellars, op. cit., p. 184.

24. This hyperlink was removed shortly after Del Ponte issued a report explaining the Tribunal's exoneration of NATO of any criminal conduct during the war, even before the Tribunal had conducted an investigation of possible criminal conduct, perhaps in reaction to the harsh criticism with which this hyperlink was met. See Mandel, 'Politics and Human Rights...,' op. cit., pp. 98-99.

25. Michael Scharf, 'Indicted For War Crimes, Then What?,' *Washington Post*, October 3, 1999.

26. Quoted in Hayden, 'Biased 'Justice',' pp. 560-561.

27. Quoted in Miriam Skoco and William Woodger, 'War Crimes,' in *Degraded Capability*, p. 35.

28. Former Chief Prosecutor Louise Arbour's complaints were aired by Simons in 'Proud but Concerned, Tribunal Prosecutor Leaves,' *New York Times*, September 15, 1999.

29. 'Tribunal: How It Works,' *New York Times*, February 12, 2002.

30. Marlise Simons, 'U.N. War Crimes Tribunal Steps Up Its Inquiry Into Kosovo,' *New York Times*, August 26, 1998.

31. 'War crimes court opens inquiry into Kosovo massacre,' Agence France Presse, January 17, 1999.

32. Barton Gellman, 'The Path to Crisis: How the United States and Its Allies

Went to War,' *Washington Post*, April 18, 1999; and Allan Little, 'How NATO was sucked into the Kosovo conflict,' *Sunday Telegraph* (London), February 27, 2000.

33. Quoted in Skoco and Woodger, op. cit., p. 35. Of course, it may be true that Arbour considered the information 'corroborated' by the simple fact that NATO offered it to her. But if true, Arbour's independence dissipates into nothing.

34. Marlise Simons, 'Militia Leader Arkan Is Indicted For War Crimes,' *New York Times*, April 1, 1999.

35. Sellars, op. cit., pp. 183-184.

36. Marcus McGee, 'Doubts Raised Over Impartiality of Prosecutor,' *Globe and Mail*, April 21, 1999.

37. As U.S. Secretary of State Madeleine Albright explained the significance of the Tribunal's indictment of Milosevic for Kosovo at a news conference on May 27, 1999: '[T]his is an important step forward and it will, one, make very clear to the world and the publics in our countries that this is justified because of the crimes committed, and I think also will enable us to keep moving all these processes forward, as I have said now, the idea of continuing with the air campaign, dealing with the humanitarian situation and also following through on various diplomatic ideas.' 'Madeleine Albright Holds Media Availability with Canadian Minister of Foreign Affairs Axworthy,' FDCH Political Transcripts, May 27, 1999.

The Tribunal's indictment of Milosevic *et al.* for alleged crimes committed in the Serbian province of Kosovo is remarkable for another little acknowledged reason: With the exception of the charges that pertain to the alleged massacre of 40-45 ethnic Albanians in and around the village of Racak, all of the other alleged crimes covered by the indictment occurred *after* the start of NATO's war on March 24, 1999. In essence, this meant that the Tribunal tried thereby to grant the NATO powers not only the *de jure* pretext for waging a non-U.N.-approved, and aggressive, war against another sovereign state, but that the target of this war, the rump Yugoslavia, would be uniquely charged with a litany of crimes for which NATO leaders were exempt by virtue of politically-based selectivity. See *The Prosecutor of the Tribunal Against Slobodan Milosevic et al., Initial Indictment [for Kosovo]*, Case No. IT-99-37, May 22, 1999, <http://www.un.org/icty/indictment/english/mil-ii990524e.htm>, as well as both subsequent *Amended Indictments*.

38. Hedging its conclusion, Human Rights Watch declared NATO guilty of violations of international humanitarian law, while Amnesty International charged NATO with crimes of war for its bombing of civilian targets. See Human Rights Watch, *Civilian Deaths in the NATO Air Campaign*, February 6, 2000, <http://www.hrw.org/reports/2000/nato/>; Amnesty International, *'Collateral Damage' or Unlawful Killings?*, June 6, 2000, <http://web.amnesty.org/library/index/ENGEUR700182000>. For an analysis of NATO's 'humanitarian' intervention as a war of aggression, see the *Memorandum*

submitted by Professor Ian Brownlie CBE, QC to the Foreign Affairs Committee of the British House of Commons, May 23, 2000, <http://www.parliament.the-stationery-office.co.uk/pa/cm199900/cmselect/cmfaff/28/28ap03.htm>.
39. 'CRISIS IN THE BALKANS; Prosecutor's Statement: 'Sufficient Evidence',' *New York Times*, May 28, 1999.
40. 'By her statement, the "chief prosecutor" has tried to act as a surrogate politician and to influence political events in the interest of the NATO countries presently waging war against Yugoslavia.' Hans Koechler, 'Illegal Tribunal – Illegal Indictment,' April 23, 2001, <http://emperors-clothes.com/docs/prog2.htm>. Koechler has served as the President of the International Progress Organization, an NGO that has worked with the United Nations for many years.
41. As Tribunal President Antonio Cassese once explained, 'The indictment means that these gentlemen will not be able to participate in peace negotiations....The politicians may not give a damn, but I'm relying on the pressure of public opinion.' Quoted in 'Karadzic A Pariah, Says War Crimes Tribunal Chief,' ANP English News Bulletin, July 27, 1995.
42. Thornberry, op. cit., p. 74.
43. As John Laughland observes: 'We now think of Nuremberg mainly as the trial of the Holocaust. This is not how the architects of Nuremberg saw matters. Exhausted by up to six years of all-engulfing war, the allies were mainly preoccupied with the fact that Nazi Germany had plunged the whole world into conflict....For the judges at Nuremberg, the primordial war crime was to start a war in the first place. All other war crimes flowed from this. Although naked aggression has always been illegal under customary international law - as is attested by the numerous and no doubt spurious legal justifications made throughout history by belligerent states for their actions - Nuremberg was innovatory in its clear legal formulation that the planning and execution of a war of aggression constituted a criminal act in international law. It was for this crime, and not for crimes against humanity, that all the Nazis at Nuremberg were judged.' 'This is not justice: The Hague has replaced Nuremberg's jurisprudence of peace with a licence to the west to kill,' *The Guardian* (London), February 16, 2002.
44. For a copy of the *Updated Statute of the International Criminal Tribunal for the Former Yugoslavia* (November, 2003), see <http://www.un.org/icty/legaldoc/index.htm>.
45. For a copy of the document filed by Michael Mandel et al. before the ICTY, requesting that the Prosecution investigate NATO-bloc officials for serious violations of international humanitarian law that fall within the jurisdiction of the Tribunal, May 6, 1999, see <http://jurist.law.pitt.edu/icty.htm>.
46. Mandel, 'Politics and Human Rights...,' op. cit., p. 95.
47. Ibid, p. 95.
48. *Final Report to the Prosecutor by the Committee Established to Review the NATO Bombing Campaign Against the Federal Republic of Yugoslavia*, U.N Doc. PR/P.I.S./510-

A Study in Propaganda

E [2000], <http://www.un.org/icty/pressreal/nato061300.htm>. (*OTP Report* hereinafter.)
49. Ibid, par. 53.
50. BBC Newsnight, February 12, 2002.
51. *OTP Report*, op. cit., pars. 59-61.
52. Mandel, op. cit., pp. 117-118.
53. 'UN war crimes tribunal focusing on commanders and leaders in Kosovo,' Agence France Press, September 29, 1999.
54. Announcing that its 'forensic program has been successfully completed,' Carla Del Ponte stated that investigators had 'found the remains of some 4,000 victims.' 'Statement to the Press by Carla Del Ponte,' FH/P.I.S./550-E, December 20, 2000, <http://www.un.org/icty/latest/index.htm>.
55. Kinkel's charge that the Serbs were the 'main source of the evil' in the conflict, that their 'ruthless war aimed at creating an ethnically cleansed greater Serbia,' and that they were committing 'genocide' in the process, first surfaced in late August, 1992, in the days leading up to the International Conference on Yugoslavia in London. See Patrick Moser, 'Peace conference on Yugoslavia opens in London,' United Press International, August 26, 1992.
56. Elaine Sciolino, 'U.S. Names Figures It Wants Charged with War Crimes,' *New York Times*, December 17, 1992. See also Johnstone, op. cit., pp. 73-74.
57. Geoffrey Robertson, *Crimes Against Humanity: The Struggle for Global Justice* (New York: The New Press, 2000), p. 301. 'Frustrating as it was for the judges to wait for suspects to fall into a net that NATO was not prepared to cast,' Robertson adds, 'it was inappropriate for [Cassese] to demand their arrest in language which suggested he had made up his mind about their guilt.'
58. 'Nasir Oric's war trophies don't line the wall of his comfortable apartment,' the *Washington Post*'s John Pomfret once reported. 'They're on a videocassette tape: burned Serb houses and headless Serb men, their bodies crumpled in a pathetic heap.' 'Weapons, Cash and Chaos Lend Clout to Srebrenica's Tough Guy,' February 16, 1994.
59. Oric was not indicted until March 28, 2003, and then only on charges related to 'violations of the laws and customs of war,' the least grave among the hierarchy of violations for which the ICTY can bring charges – but not 'crimes against humanity,' and certainly not 'genocide.' See *The Prosecutor of the Tribunal Against Naser Oric, Amended Indictment*, Case No. IT-03-68-PT, July 16, 2003, <http://www.un.org/icty/indictment/english/ori-ii030328e.htm>.
60. *The Prosecutor of the Tribunal Against Milan Martic, Initial Indictment*, Case No. IT-95-11, July 25, 1995, par. 7; pars. 15-18, <http://www.un.org/icty/indictment/english/mar-ii950725e.htm>; and Hayden, 'Biased 'Justice',' pp. 573-575.
61. Marlise Simons, 'General Gets 20 Years for Sarajevo Atrocities,' *New York Times*, December 6, 2003.
62. *The Prosecutor of the Tribunal Against Ante Gotovina*, Case No. IT-01/45-I, <http://www.un.org/icty/indictment/english/got-ii010608e.htm>.

63. On the presence of the Mujahedin as well as mercenary and other forces tied to (largely American) military-related corporations in Bosnia, see Cees Wiebes, *Intelligence and the War in Bosnia 1992-1995* (London: Lit Verlag, 2003), Ch. 4, 'Secret Arms Supplies and Other Covert Operations,' esp. pp. 207-208.

64. Following the deaths of Franjo Tudjman (December 10, 1999) and Alija Izetbegovic (October 19, 1003), the Office of the Prosecutor claimed that both men had been under investigation for possible indictment for actions taken during their wartime leaderships. Of course, in neither case was an indictment ever produced; and in both instances, the deaths of these two figures permanently closed their cases. On Tudjman, see 'Tudjman buried Monday,' Agence France Presse, December 13, 1999; and Beth Potter, 'Court: Tudjman indictment was discussed,' United Press International, December 14, 1999; and on Izetbegovic, see 'U.N. prosecutors were investigating former Bosnian president Izetbegovic,' Associated Press, October 22, 2003; and Stephen Castle, 'Bosnian Leader Was Suspected of War Crimes,' *The Independent* (London), October 23, 2003.

65. Marlise Simons, 'Militia Leader Arkan Is Indicted for War Crimes,' *New York Times*, April 1, 1999.

66. In only one bylined article has Marlise Simons ever mentioned the name 'Naser Oric': Namely, on April 12, 2003, a 124-word blurb in the World Briefing Europe section titled, 'The Netherlands: Bosnian Muslim To U.N. Tribunal.' Because of its brevity, this article failed to make the Simons Universe. See n. 6, above.

67. Although Simons published no article on the subject at the time of the May 22 indictment, she did take up the matter in a retrospective profile of Louise Arbour, 'Proud But Concerned, Tribunal Prosecutor Leaves,' *New York Times*, September 15, 1999.

68. Stephen Lee Myers, 'Kosovo Inquiry Confirms U.S. Fears of War Crimes Court,' *New York Times*, January 3, 2000.

69. Marlise Simons, 'General Clark to Testify for the Prosecution at Milosevic Trial,' *New York Times*, December 14, 2003.

70. Marlise Simons, 'An Unexpected Reversal Of War Crimes Convictions: U.N. Panel Shows It's Not a Rubber Stamp,' *New York Times*, October 29, 2001.

71. See the analysis in Koechler, op. cit.

72. Quoted in George Szamuely, 'US Hypocrisy on Those IKCs – You Guessed It, International Kangaroo Courts,' *CounterPunch*, September 24, 2002, <http://www.counterpunch.com.szamuely0924.html>.

73. Michael Mandel, 'Milosevic Has a Point,' *Toronto Globe and Mail*, July 6, 2001, <http://www.commondreams.org/views01/0706-05.htm>.

74. Statement by Antonio Cassese to the Secretary General of the United Nations on January 21, 1994; quoted in Christopher Black, 'An Impartial Tribunal? Really?,' November 21, 1999, <http://emperors-clothes.com/analysis/Impartial.htm>.

A Study in Propaganda

75. Hayden, 'Biased 'Justice',' p. 569.
76. 'When asked by U.S. Information Agency pollsters what they feel are the most urgent issues facing their country,' Charles Boyd reports, 'Croats, Muslims, and Serbs have consistently ranked bringing war criminals to justice near the bottom. No more than six percent of the members of any faction regarded the issue as important.' 'Making Bosnia Work,' *Foreign Affairs*, January/February, 1998, p. 51. Boyd is a retired U.S. Air Force General with experience in the Balkans.
77. On the vetting process for the judges who have served on the ICTY's bench, see Mandel, *How America Gets Away With Murder*, Ch. 4; and Carol Off, *The Lion, the Fox and the Eagle* (Canada: Random House Canada, 2000), p. 279ff.
78. Koechler, op. cit.
79. Sellars, op. cit., p. 186.
80. Quoted in Black, op. cit.
81. Quoted in John Laughland, "The anomalies of the International Criminal Tribunal are legion...',' *The Times* (London), June 17, 1999.
82. Ibid.
83. Ibid.
84. Robertson, op. cit., p. 418. He adds that although Arbour was surely 'grateful' for the help, she was 'unwise to take photo opportunities with Mr. Cook and the belligerent NATO general, Wesley Clark, which cast a shadow over her impartiality' – neglecting the fact that there was no other reason for Arbour to have made this trip in the first place, but to enhance the public image of the NATO-ICTY partnership, and the justness of NATO's 'bombing for humanity' (Robertson's phrase).
85. 'Another achievement of the tribunals has been to marginalize indicted war criminals who have not yet been arrested,' Richard J. Goldstone explains, citing as prime examples the July 1995 indictments of Radovan Karadzic and Ratko Mladic, and the May 1999 indictment of Slobodan Milosevic. *For Humanity: Reflections of a War Crimes Investigator* (New Haven: Yale University Press, 2000), p. 126.
86. Marlise Simons, 'War Crimes Tribunal Expands Milosevic Indictment,' *New York Times*, June 30, 2001. The *Times* later reported that in an interview that the French daily newspaper *Le Monde* published on the morning of Milosevic's first appearance before the Tribunal, July 3, 2001, to hear the charges against him for alleged crimes in Kosovo, Del Ponte announced that 'she envisages bringing charges of genocide against Milosevic for Serbian crimes in the Bosnian and Croatian wars.' Roger Cohen and Marlise Simons, 'At Arraignment, Milosevic Scorns His U.N. Accusers,' July 4, 2001.
87. ANP English News Bulletin, op. cit.
88. Quoted in Skoco and Woodger, op. cit., p. 37.
89. According to Simons, 'Investigators at the Hague are notoriously discreet about their inquiries and rarely allow their names to be used.' 'Case Against

Milosevic Is Not Simple to Prove,' *New York Times*, July 2, 2001.
90. Hayden, 'Biased 'Justice',' p. 562.
91. Ibid., p. 567.
92. Ibid., p. 568.
93. Marlise Simons, 'Far From Former Yugoslavia, First War Crimes Trial Opens,' *New York Times*, May 8, 1996.
94. David Owen, *Balkan Odyssey* (New York: Harcourt Brace, 1995).
95. For Robert Hayden's testimony, see *The Prosecutor of the Tribunal Against Dusko Tadic a/k/a 'Dule' a/k/a/ 'Dusan' [and] Goran Borovnica*, Case No. IT-94-1-T, Transcripts, September 10, 1996, pp. 5590-5648, <http://www.un.org/icty/transe1/960910ed.htm>; and September 11, 1996, pp. 5649-5792, <http://www.un.org/icty/transe1/960911IT.htm>.
96. Marlise Simons, 'Civil, It Wasn't; Defining a War to Determine the Crime,' *New York Times*, May 18, 1997.
97. Marlise Simons, 'Balkan Rivals Revive Past in Icy Face-Off At U.N. Trial,' *New York Times*, May 22, 2003.
98. As one of the courtroom *amicus* lawyers for Milosevic, Branislav Tapuskovic, complained before the start of Milosevic's cross-examination of Kucan, 'to bring in a key witness of this nature for only one day is not sufficient.' But just as clearly, this judgment depends on what the prosecution intended Kucan's single-day's worth of testimony to be sufficient for. See 'Kosovo, Croatia and Bosnia,' Case IT-02-54, May 21, 2003, p. 20904, <http://www.un.org/icty/transe54/030521ED.htm>.
99. Op cit., p. 20915 and *passim*.
100. See Woodward, op. cit., pp. 134-143. Woodward also notes that 'whatever the army did was automatically labeled as pro-Serb' (p. 137). The level of distrust and violence directed against the JNA in the period before and after Slovenia's and Croatia's declarations of independence is seldom appreciated.
101. 'Kosovo, Croatia and Bosnia,' op cit., p. 20923ff.
102. Op cit., p. 20947.
103. Op cit., p. 20948ff.
104. Simons, 'Balkan Rivals....' Evidently, Kucan fared far worse in the judgment of the Office of the Prosecutor. One little known fact, also unreported by the *New York Times*, was the prosecution's last-minute rush to call the Slovenian legal expert and former member of the Yugoslav Constitutional Court, Ivan Kristan, to testify just two days after Kucan, hopefully to counter the damage stemming from Kucan's appearance. BBC Monitoring International Reports, May 22, 2003, reproducing a report by the STA News Agency, Ljubljana, May 22, 2003. (Logistic delays would prevent Kristan from testifying until September 1, 2003.)
105. Anthony Deutsch, 'Ex-Yugoslav President Backs Milosevic,' Associated Press, June 17, 2003; Stephanie Van Den Berg, 'Milosevic not linked to Srebrenica massacre: former Yugo President,' Agence France Presse, June 17, 2003.

106. Marlise Simons, 'Prosecutors Say Documents Link Milosevic to Genocide,' *New York Times*, June 20, 2003.
107. 'Kosovo, Croatia and Bosnia,' Case IT-02-54, November 19, 2003, p. 29215ff; pp. 29314-29315, <http://www.un.org/icty/transe54/031119ED.htm>.
108. 'Kosovo, Croatia and Bosnia,' Case IT-02-54, November 20, 2003, pp. 29341-19343, <http://www.un.org/icty/transe54/031120IT.htm>.
109. See the *Initial Indictment [for Bosnia-Herzegovina]*, Case No. IT-01-51-I, November 22, 2001, par. 7; *First Amended Indictment of Milosevic [for Croatia]*, Case No. IT-02-54-T, October 27, 2002, par. 7.
110. Toby Sterling, 'Milosevic gives foretaste of defense in cross-examination of former ally,' Associated Press Worldstream, November 19, 2003.
111. Note that through the date of this writing, the Tribunal in fact has never announced any indictment of Borisav Jovic.
112. Marlise Simons, 'Milosevic Is Ill; Trial May Slow,' *New York Times*, July 26, 2002.
113. Marlise Simons, 'Milosevic Finds a Friendly Face In the Witness Stand at His Trial,' *New York Times*, July 27, 2002.
114. Cedric Thornberry, wondering at the overwhelming and selective focus on Serb crimes, says that 'a kindly soul at U.N. headquarters in New York, ear to the diplomatic grapevine, warned me in the spring of 1993, 'Take cover – the fix is on.' Op. cit., pp. 78-79.
115. Marlise Simons, 'Plea Deals Being Used to Clear Balkan War Tribunal's Docket,' *New York Times*, November 18, 2003.
116. Marlise Simons, 'Officers Say Bosnian Massacre Was Deliberate,' *New York Times*, October 12, 2003.
117. Ibid.
118. Greenspan, op. cit.
119. Ian Johnson, 'The Judge As Prosecutor: Two Days At The "Trial" of Slobodan Milosevic,' June 19, 2002, <http://www.icdsm.org/more/days-i.htm>.
120. See Mandel, *How America Gets Away With Murder*, Ch. 5.
121. See 'Kosovo, Croatia and Bosnia,' Case IT-02-54, February 18, 2002, p. 523, <http://www.un.org/icty/transe54/020218IT.htm>.
122. The estimate is Michael Scharf's, as quoted in Sellars, op. cit., p. 187.
123. *Rules of Procedure and Evidence*, Rule 96, Evidence in Cases of Sexual Assault, December 17, 2003, <www.un.org/icty/basic/rpe/IT32_rev19.htm#Rule96>.
124. When Wesley Clark testified in the Milosevic trial, the *Times*'s editors turned their paper's coverage over to Simons' colleague, Elaine Sciolino, who filed three reports on the testimony: 'Clark Testifies Against Milosevic at Hague Tribunal,' December 16, 2003; 'Milosevic Trial Helps Clark Try To Gain Notice,' December 17, 2003; 'Clark Testimony Links Milosevic Directly to '95 Massacre,' December 19, 2003. Like Simons, Sciolino's reports never once deviated from the party-line.
125. Tiphaine Dickson, 'Protesting Wesley Clark: As Saddam Faces War Crimes

Trial, Milosevic's Kangaroo Court Hops to US Orders,' *Counterpunch*, December 1-15, 2003; Paul Mitchell, 'Milosevic trial sets precedent: US granted right to censor,' December 31, 2003, <http://www.wsws.org/articles/2003/dec2003/cens-d31_prn.shtml>.

126. Marlise Simons, 'Judges at War Crimes Trial Rein in Milosevic,' *New York Times*, September 22, 2003.

127. Marlise Simons, 'Milosevic Trial Settles Into Slow But Judicious Routine,' *New York Times*, March 3, 2003.

128. Ian Traynor, 'War Crimes Suspects May Avoid Trial,' *The Guardian* (London), February 11, 2004.

129. For example, it was regularly acknowledged during the Vietnam war that the successive rulers of South Vietnam, from Ngo Dinh Diem in 1954 to Nugen Van Thieu in 1974, all of whom were imposed (and some removed) by U.S. officials, could not possibly compete with the Communists on a purely political basis, and were wholly dependent on U.S. support. Nevertheless, these same Saigon puppets were often annoyed that U.S. officials failed to treat them with the respect due independent rulers, although the U.S. media came close to doing that.

130. John Dewey *et al*., *Not Guilty: Report of the Commission of Inquiry Into the Charges Made Against Leon Trotsky in the Moscow Trials*, 2nd. Ed. (New York: Monad Press, 1972).

131. Ibid, p. 393.

132. Ibid, p. 19; p. 388.

133. Ibid, p. xxi; p. 21.

134. Ibid, p. 25.

Forthcoming from Merlin Press

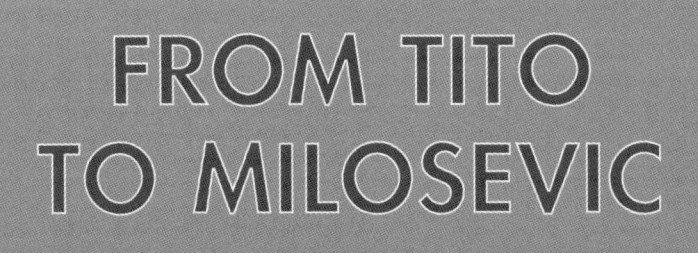

FROM TITO TO MILOSEVIC

Yugoslavia, the Lost Country

MICHAEL BARRATT BROWN

ISBN 085036552X £14.95 www.merlinpress.co.uk
Also available from
Bertrand Russell House, Bulwell Lane, Nottingham NG6 0BT

THE SPOKESMAN
Founded by Bertrand Russell

America's Gulag

Full Spectrum Dominance *versus* **Universal Human Rights**
€10 / $10 / £5

"I've just had a chance to read *The Spokesman*... it's really first-rate."
Noam Chomsky

"Read it we must." **Tony Benn**

America's Gulag
Edited by Ken Coates
James Kirkup
Bertrand Russell
Irene Khan
Dear Mr President...
Ibrahim Warde
Iraq: Looter's Licence
Kurt Vonnegut
Creative Writing
Bruce Kent
Vanunu- Free at Last
Tony Blair et al
Prisoner Abuse in Iraq
Report of the International Committee of the Red Cross
Amnesty International
Killing of Civilians in Basra and al-Amara
The Taguba Report-More Missing Pages

Dark Times: Torture

Edited by Ken Coates
Louise Christian
Experiment in Inhumanity
Lord Steyn
Guantanamo Bay: Legal Black Hole
Inge Genefke
Torture: Weapon against Democracy
Lindsey Collen & Ragini Kistnasamy
How Deigo Garcia Was Stolen
Kurt Vonnegut
State of the Asylum
Arundhati Roy
Project for a New World Communion
Noam Chomsky
Remembering History
Richard B. Du Boff
US Hegemony
Ken Coates
Iraq's Declaration: What Happened?

€10 / $10 / £5 **Dark Times**

One year's subscription to *The Spokesman* (4 issues) costs £20
(£25, €40 or $40 ex UK) Credit/Debit cards accepted
(VISA, Mastercard, Switch, Delta, Electron & Solo)
Spokesman Books, (LRB) Russell House, Bulwell Lane,
Nottingham, NG6 0BT, England
Tel: 0115 9708318 - **Fax:** 0115 9420433
e-mail: elfeuro@compuserve.com - www.spokesmanbooks.com